BRUNO MUGNAI

FOREIGN VOLUNTEERS AND INTERNATIONAL BRIGADES IN THE SPANISH CIVIL WAR (1936-39)

SOLDIERS&WEAPONS 006

SOLDIERSHOP PUBLISHING

ABOUT THE AUTHOR

Bruno Mugnai was born in Florence in 1962 and lives there with Silvia, Chiara and Eugenio. Passionate about military history since he was very young, he has published two books on the Ottoman Army from 1645 to 1718. He is also the author of essays on the Italian campaign of the Spanish War of Succession and articles of uniformity and military history of the seventeenth and eighteenth centuries. More recently, he has treated the military history of Tuscany during the French revolutionary campaigns, the Napoleonic era and the pre-unification era. He has also published a monograph on the military institutions of the Italian Army of the State of Lucca in the 19th century for the Historical Office of the Italian Army and has completed for the same editorial a similar contribution on the army of the Grand Duchy of Tuscany from 1737 to 1799. With Luca Cristini he has collaborated in the illustrations of the two volumes dedicated to the War of the 30 Years and to the realization of Soldiershop's *L'Esercito Imperiale al tempo del principe Eugenio di Savoia; la fanteria*.

EDITORIAL NOTE

A large part of the images featured on our books, publications and prints -in the case of not being part of our unpublished creations- are taken from copies of first editions or from books that have not been restricted by copyright for a long time, and, therefore, they are in the public domain. We are a specialized publisher and therefore we have, or have had, the availability of numerous old and ancient books and texts whose copyrights have already expired. Several images, in addition, are the result of our complete graphic recreation, carried out by expert artists in military illustration. Consequently, all the images and texts of our books, in any format (paper, electronic or other), are the property of Soldiershop.com. The translation, reproduction, or copy rights by any means, digital, photographic, photocopy, etc. are reserved to all countries. None of the images in our books can be reproduced without the written permission of Soldiershop.com. We kindly inform interested readers that a good part of the original works produced by our artists are available for sale to individuals. However, we must point that also in such cases the reproduction rights remain the property of Soldiershop.com. The editor will always be available to address any person who believes they have found a dubious or unidentified source. For any request write to info@soldiershop.com. The marks @Soldiershop Publishing, @Bookmoon and the names of our collections *Soldiers & Weapons, Battlefield, War in colour, Paper Soldiers, Soldiershop e-Books* are property of Soldiershop.com; consequently, its external use is not allowed.

SOLDIERS & WEAPONS

It is the main and most important of all our series, dedicated to military history, the uniforms and weapons of the armies involved in the great wars of the past. Created by a team of renowned historians and illustrators, it consists of books of approximately 70 pages each, with dozens of excellent colour illustrations. The collection is characterized by a horizontal dark blue line on the cover.

PUBLISHING'S NOTES

None of unpublished images or text of our book may be reproduced in any format without the expressed written permission of Soldiershop.com when not indicate as marked with license creative commons 3.0 or 4.0. Soldiershop Publishing has made every reasonable effort to locate, contact and acknowledge rights holders and to correctly apply terms and conditions to Content. In the event that any Content infringes your rights or the rights of any third parties, or Content is not properly identified or acknowledged we would like to hear from you so we may make any necessary alterations. In this event contact: info@soldiershop.com. Our trademark: Soldiershop Publishing @, The names of our series & brand: Museum book, Bookmoon, Soldiers&Weapons, Battlefield, War in colour, Historical Biographies, Darwin's view, Fabula, Altrastoria, Italia Storica Ebook, Witness To History, Soldiers, Weapons & Uniforms, Storia etc. are herein @ by Soldiershop.com.

LICENSES COMMONS

This book may utilize part of material marked with license creative commons 3.0 or 4.0 (CC BY 4.0), (CC BY-ND 4.0), (CC BY-SA 4.0) or (CC0 1.0). Or derived from publication 70 years old or more and recolored from us. We give appropriate attribution credit and indicate if change were made in the acknowledgements field.
All our books utilize only fonts licensed under the SIL Open Font License or other free use license.

ISBN: 9788893274210 3rd Edition in English: April 2019
Title: FOREIGN VOLUNTEERS AND INTERNATIONAL BRIGADES IN THE SPANISH CIVIL WAR (1936-39)
by Bruno Mugnai
Editor: Soldiershop Publishing. Photo coloration: Luca S. Cristini, Anna Cristini y Joel Bellviure.
Traslate by Joel Bellviure
Cover: Volunteers of the International Brigades (author's design)

INTRODUCTION

By the late seventies, it was reckoned that at least 20,000 books about the Spanish Civil War had been published and, of these, around a hundred were about international volunteers. Twenty years later, Andy Durgan, in his article *Freedom fighters or Comintern army? The International Brigades in Spain*, doubled these figures, a sign that the debate had not concluded, and that works were still being written by integrating precedents and adding new data thanks to research carried out in the Comintern archives or in other political organizations. This contribution is, therefore, part of the broad context of publications on foreign combatants in the Civil War. It has been especially created to fill a void still present, that of the military history of the Italian volunteers, being aware that similar contributions have already appeared for a long time, but that have almost always privileged the International Brigades and, within these, the British and North American formations.

These are historically interesting, but of relative numerical consistency, having been treated more frequently, while Italian volunteers became the third largest component among the *internacionales*. Without any doubt, is not one of the goals of this book to present a new interpretation of the events, but, on the other hand, it is impossible to approach the facts while ignoring the erroneous decisions and mistakes made within the Antifascist side. Seventy years after these events, it is still difficult to reliably reconstruct the facts and background that determined, even among foreign volunteers, tragedies and lacerations in the formation of the units.

These disappointed many of those who had come to fight and that, eventually, led to the defeat of the Republic. All this has contributed to make responsibilities unclear, while other times some realities have been manipulated and certain convictions among historians have survived, both claimed from the right and left wing. We often find these distortions when we examine the history of volunteer units, such as the belief that the International Brigades contributed to the repression of Anarchists and Trotskyists in Barcelona in May 1937.

Another dogma that needs to be discredited is that foreign volunteers were part only of the International Brigades, when this phenomenon was carried out throughout the Republican deployment, in specific units within the Anarchist organizations, recently object of a very interesting and relevant investigation for the adequate understanding of the surrounding studies of international antifascism in Spain. In the first stage of the war, for example, some of the most important exponents of Italian antifascism in exile, such as Carlo Rosselli, Camillo Berneri, and many others, acted in prominent positions. It is appropriate, therefore, to separate the history of the voluntary formations that arose at the beginning of the war from the epic of the International Brigades. For the author it must not have been easy to analyse the sources, ideologically conditioned and, therefore, partial. It seems to us, therefore, a great merit not only to have reconstructed some of the fundamental aspects of these units, as their effective contribution to the struggle, how the formation of the official units occurred, or to what extent the ideology contributed to the discipline of the units, from which arose the argument of the "internal democracy" of the *milicias* -the proletarian army that used methods other than those of the other armies.

And, considering that this last concept, more than others, has always generated heated debates, it is very likely that it will remain forever as a myth.

Luca Cristini

SUMMARY:

1ST CHAPTER - INTERNATIONAL VOLUNTEERS .... Pag. 5
The first international units of the *Milicia Popular*
Communist and Socialist international units
Anarchist international units
POUM international units - Epilogue.

2ND CHAPTER - INTERNATIONAL BRIGADES .... Pag. 23
Equipment - Organization, logistcs and training - Brigade in action -
The war campaign: XI Brigade, XII Brigade, XIII Brigade, XIV Brigade, XV Brigade,
LXXXVI Brigade, CXXIX Brigade, XI Brigade, CL Brigade, Balance.

NOTES TO COLOUR PLATES .... Pag. 69
BIBLIOGRAPHY .... Pag. 81

▼ In the middle, American writer Ernest Hemingway, visiting the International Brigades headquarters, and, on the right, Arnold Friedrich Vieth von Golsseneau, alias Ludwig Renn, since November 1936, chief of Staff of the XI Brigade, in a photo taken at the beginning of 1937. Renn wears an old Spanish Army officer regular uniform, replaced at the end of 1936 by a new one, distinguished by a single-breasted jacket with an open lapel at the neck and new rank insignia. On the left, Dutch director Joris Ivens. (Deutsches Bundesarchiv, Allgemeiner Deut. Nachrichtendienst, 183-84600-0001).

1. INTERNATIONAL VOLUNTEERS

"It was in Spain where my generation learned that one can be right and yet be beaten, that force can vanquish spirit, and that sometimes courage does not get any recompense." (Albert Camus)

INTRODUCTION

Although more than sixty years have passed since the end of the Spanish Civil War, the historical and political debate finds itself continually fed by new contributions, especially after the archives of the former USSR were opened to researchers. Much of the more recent literature offers, and sometimes denies, new reconstructions of those facts, a sign that the debate is not over yet, neither in Spain nor in the rest of the world. Although today there is no doubt that the largest number of volunteers came from Communist organizations around the world, the contribution of those who did not recognize themselves within the Marxist-Leninist ideology, especially Italians, is increasingly more evident. There were also many Socialists, Anarchists, Republicans, and members of other Antifascist organizations, such as Giustizia e Libertà. According to current estimates, the total number of Italian volunteers not adhering to the Third International would have been between 35% and 40% of the total. Also, regarding the total number of volunteers who went to Spain, we face a subject that confronted many authors, often reaching different conclusions, not so much in relation to their total, but rather on their political affiliation, emphasizing only the data useful to support their theses. Other arguments, sometimes presented in an instrumental way, tend to highlight the participation of some nationalities or ethnic groups and then, on the basis of this fact, if it is established that the French and Germans represented more than a third of the entire international contingent, it is equally true that arriving in Spain was much easier for those residing in France and that, in any case, together with Germany, these were countries with a large population and a tradition of consolidated political struggle. Therefore, in relation to proximity, the total number of inhabitants and the strength of the respective left parties, the small but fierce group of fighters from countries such as Albania or Estonia, or even from very distant countries, such as the relatively scarce but certainly motivated volunteers from Australia and New Zealand acquire a very different value. Finally, if we compare the number of volunteers with the population of each state, it is the Cubans who, surprisingly, earn the primacy of the most represented nationality. The controversy over the responsibilities of the European and Stalinist democratic governments is an important part of the enormous mass of books on the Civil War, and, although their histories do not form the main part of these works, practically all the authors have mentioned the foreign volunteers, something that would be difficult to avoid, given the propaganda campaign that accompanied the International Brigades and their participation in the conflict.

If this has magnified the deforming lens with which the vicissitudes of foreign volunteers have been read, it is still impossible to ignore the historical fact that involved the mobilization of a considerable number of men and women of different nationalities who, under the name of democracy, ran to Spain ready to sacrifice their lives for a country that was not theirs. In the ocean of mistakes, disappointments and contradictions in which so many volunteers found themselves acting -consciously, reluctantly, or openly at odds with the government they defended- the internacionales still represent one of the strongest symbols of class solidarity and brotherhood among nations.

INTERNATIONAL VOLUNTEERS

Immediately after the Rebel generals' coup, the first armed formations that supported the Republican Government gathered around their political organizations. In Catalonia, in particular, among the most radical movements an intense activity was recorded. It formed a fierce contingent of volunteers in a very short time, ready to take action and counteract the insurgency. But the first foreigners to join the Republican line-up were in Spain for other reasons. In fact, in a few days, it was planned that, in Barcelona, took place the anti-Olympic games of the working class, the so-called Spartakiad, who had gathered in the city a good number of "proletarian athletes", coaches and companions to participate in these Games organized in opposition to the Olympic Games of Berlin. It is estimated that at least 300 young foreigners who had to take part in the event joined militia formations at the end of July 1936, which constitutes the first group of international volunteers in Spain. An article published in the Journal of Catalan Reformist Socialists said that, in Barcelona, between July 18 to 20, during the clashes 'the German Antifascist' Johann Frey and the Austrian Franz Mechter lost their lives, while among the wounded they found the students Rudolph Kohn of Germany and the Italians Paolo Girelli, worker of Brescia, and the 'athlete Bruno Serene'. During the first stages of the Civil War, the volunteer recruitment followed the recruits' own political affiliation, so some adhered to the militias of the PSOE and the UGT (Unión General de Trabajadores, General Union of Workers), and others to the JSU (Joventuts Socialistes Unificades, Unified Socialist Youths), the POUM (Partido Obrero de Unificación Marxista, Workers' Party of Marxist Unification), the CNT (Conferración Nacional de Trabajadores, National Confederation of Labour) or the Fifth Regiment (Quinto Regimiento), an armed group formed by members of the Socialist-Communist Youth of the PCE

(Partido Comunista Español, Communist Party of Spain). In fact, this was the only party within the governmental group that had close contacts with the Communist International, and in a short time proved to have a branched and very efficient organizational structure; although, in 1936, the Communists of strict Soviet militancy were a small contingent in Spain. In the Fifth Regiment the Italian Communist Vittorio Vidali, better known under the war name of "Carlos Contreras", carried out his duties since the summer of 1936, and introduced the structure and the strict disciplinary methods of the Soviet Army in the unit. Later, Vidali would take high positions in the International Brigades, obtaining the grade of political commissar and director of the infamous internal counterintelligence. Although the Soviet Union represented an indispensable point of reference for many Communists, the consensus towards Moscow was not the same everywhere. The first Germans who arrived at Spain were united by indignation at Stalin's reluctance to unleash a revolution in Germany. For this reason, the groups of volunteers exiled from the Nazi regime originally formed two distinct groups. The first was created on August 7 by members loyal to the Moscow party, under the command of Albert Schreiner and named after the Communist leader Ernst Thaelmann, imprisoned by the Nazis in Hamburg in 1933. The second group was created around the figure of Hans Beimler, former Communist MP of the Reichstag, protagonist of a legendary escape from a concentration camp, but considered rather opposed to Stalin's directives. This second group included over sixty Germans together several Danes and Swedes. From the merger of these formations, which took place at the end of August, the Thaelmann Centuria (a unit of 100 men, hence the name) was born. Of the strength of a small battalion, it was characterized, like all proletarian and popular militias, by an improvised armament but counteracted by a determination soon to become proverbial. Before the formation was established, another Thaelmann group, without any relation with the one created in August, was formed in Barcelona on July 23, 1936 by 11 German exiles, 8 men and 3 women, who joined the columns of militiamen in Aragón. After the Germans, the Italian volunteers represented the second major group of exiles, who rushed in large numbers from neighbouring France and Switzerland. On August 3, 1936, in the press around Barcelona, it was mentioned for the first time the formation of Italian volunteers, referring to an Italian group within the 19 de July Column (or battalion),

▲ Turinese Socialist Fernando De Rosa was in exile in Spain long before 1936, after having served four years in prison in Belgium for having tried to shoot Umberto di Savoia with a gun. From July 1936, De Rosa was head of the October Battalion of the militia of the Partido Socialista Obrero Español (Spanish Socialist Workers' Party, PSOE), which he commanded during the clashes that preceded the siege of Madrid. He was one of the first Italian Antifascists who fell during the Civil War. The presence of foreigners with military experience was considered very useful by the Republican Government. In July 1936, forces on the front seemed balanced, with approximately 30,000 men on each side, although of the more than 11,000 officers, more than 7,000 were aligned with the rebels and, of the remaining, only a thousand, including thirty generals, were considered up to the situation. (Illustration of a post-war poster in memory of Fernando De Rosa, Author's archive)

belonging to the militia of the PSUC (Partit Socialista Unificat de Catalunya, Unified Socialist Party of Catalonia), the Catalan political organization adhered to the Comintern, the organism that met the parties of the III International. Probably, these volunteers belonged to the Italian community already present in Barcelona, which was joined by an "athlete" of the Spartakiad. Other Italians living in Barcelona, often known to the Fascist authorities, showed considerable prominence since the early days of the military uprising, such as the anarchist Artorige Nozzoli, hatter and former legionario of the Tercio, who appeared in all demonstrations against the Falangists and participated in all the assemblies of the CNT in Barcelona. An informant of the Italian police informed Rome that 'you can see Nozzoli strolling the streets of Barcelona armed with a gun and an old chivalry sword. Encourages, cheers, makes plans and ruses for attacks and raids against Falangists, Fascists, etc. and uses the anarchist uniform'. Among the first to arrive in Spain after the news of an uprising, the French were a significant exception, since the local leftist organizations were able to establish voluntary formations in their territory. The first group was established in Bordeaux and included French and Belgians. Once in Spain, it took the name of Commune de Paris Centuria and joined the militia of the PCE. Since August it was under the orders of Jules Dumont, an officer from the Communist Party and future leader of the resistance against the Nazis. The first French militias turned out to be those that, for obvious reasons, seemed better organized and politically more homogeneous. Moreover, it was almost always a question of contingents not opposed to the policy of the Communist International and which later would come together in the International Brigades. A small number of British Antifascists had arrived in Spain, attracted by the internationalist echo and the Republican cause. The first two volunteers were named Samuel "Sam" Masters and Nat Cohen, two London tailors who rode the country on a bicycle when the rebellion exploded. Both members of the Communist Party of Great Britain went to

Barcelona where, together with other countrymen, founded the Thomas Mann Centuria.

The group, consisting of about forty volunteers, also included the Italian Giorgio Tioli and some important names of left-wing British journalism, such as Keith Scott-Wilson and Tom Wintingrham, later official in the International Brigades, as well as seventeen-year-old Esmond Romilly, nephew of Winston Churchill, and author of a vivid account of the fighting in Madrid. The British were framed along with some local formations to participate in the unfinished expedition to Majorca, during which a volunteer was severely injured. Frustrated by the lack of action, all members of the Thomas Mann joined the German volunteers of the Thaelmann Centuria at the end of September. In the same period, many Polish Communists arrived in Spain from neighbouring France, thus creating the first volunteer units from Eastern Europe, which also included Czechs, Slovaks, Hungarians, and Yugoslavs. The populous community of Polish miners in France had massively joined the leftist movements, both reformist and revolutionary, and over time the presence of volunteers ended up coming directly from Poland. At the end of the Civil war, the Poles became one of the most numerous nationalities among the international volunteers along with the French, German and Italian. Through the many channels opened by Antifascist organizations, more and more volunteers arrived. Before the end of July, it is estimated that at least 600 volunteers arrived in Barcelona by train or by sea, united by the desire to join the militia formations to defend the Republic with weapons. These volunteers can only be considered partly as predecessors of the internacionales who would later form the Brigades. What most put them together was the blatant distrust of Moscow's politics and their indecision to intervene in support of the revolution, to the extent that the majority chose to finally fight as guerrillas in Catalonia and Aragón, along with their Spanish comrades or in other formations of the Republican Army.

THE FIRST INTERNATIONAL UNITS OF THE *MILICIA POPULAR*

Historical research has sporadically dealt with the events of the volunteers who arrived in Spain after the first news of the clashes came out, in order to participate in the revolution that erupted in Catalonia, attracted by the news about collectivization, socialization, workers' and peasants' committees, or simply to defend democracy and demonstrate that antifascism wasn't dead. The presence of these volunteers was opposed to those who claimed that only the propaganda and organization provided by Moscow could have organized the Antifascist fight in defence of the Republic. In this context, the history of those who came from Italy is among the groups that might seem particularly significant, since they were one of the first spontaneously documented in Catalan militias organized by local parties, by the most radical, as by Anarchists and moderates, as by Social Democrats and Republicans. The scenario that these volunteers found in Spain was incandescent. Regardless of what happened during the Asturian Revolution, between the February elections and the military Revolt of July 1936, 113 general strikes took place in Spain, and another 228 partial, 145 bomb attacks, 215 attacks on political headquarters, and 150 burnings of churches. Accidents caused 269 deaths and 1,287 injured. This high level of conflict was the basis of rapid growth in armed formations linked to political organizations and trade unions. Indeed, before the mid-1930s, trade unions, paramilitary structures, and almost all Republican formations had created paramilitary structures for self-defence, aware of what had happened to unions and their allied parties in Italy, Germany, and Austria. In the summer of 1936, the Republican militia was, in fact, divided into two relatively homogeneous groups: on the one hand, the formations of reformist political organizations, including those belonging to the International, such as the fierce and prestigious Fifth Regiment, those of the UGT Union of Socialist character, and the less numerous of Izquierda Republicana (Republican Left); on the other, the militias of the CNT and the other revolutionary formations. But, while among the first there was only one formal connection, between the Anarchists and the militiamen of the POUM a collaboration was established, eventually soldered in a true political alliance. It seems to be, however, that in the first months of the conflict the ideological rivalry within the Republican forces was not considered decisive and, even many months after the beginning of the war, Socialists and Republicans could be found within Anarchist formations, or Anarchists in militias of parties like the POUM and, later, even within the International Brigades. In general, however, foreign volunteers were welcome, as they were ideologically framed and considered to be very determined fighters. In addition, unlike their Spanish comrades, there was always someone with knowledge on military tactics, because of having served during the First World War. The foreign presence in the militia formations therefore assumed an incalculable importance from the moral point of view. The popular imagination led to the assessment that volunteers arriving from abroad were full combatants, hardly experienced, only because their respective countries had participated in the First World War. In fact, the "experience baggage" was ultimately the scarcest aptitude in the militia, where enthusiasm and goodwill failed to fill the gaps of military training. In the militia, methods of command and discipline were introduced, inspired by every ideology, so, in many cases, officers and NCOs were chosen among sympathizers to the dominant party, or they adapted the principles of self-discipline on councils directly run by the soldiers, as experienced in anarchist units. The formation of the broader militia unit, the columna, came from the guerrilla units of the Peninsular War against Napoleon, and reflected a horizontal military structure, in which the armed groups could converge acting in different ways. It was a model that could be perfectly adapted to the ideological and military needs of many militia formations, in which the principles of equality and those of the Assembly replaced the rules of traditional armies. On the contrary, the Communist formations linked to the Comintern were those in which a more rigid discipline was immediately adopted, similar to that of the regular units of the Army. This contrasted strongly with the rules regulating the activities of the other militias and was the basis of endless discussions between the different orientations of the Republican staff.

Between October 1936 and March of the following year, with the definitive incorporation of all the militia in the regular army, it had provided to the front of combat more than 100,000 men; almost half of them belonging to the CNT-FAI units, divided between the strongholds of Aragón, Madrid and Catalonia. Another 6,000 men -more than 2,000 in the reserve- belonged to the POUM and were on the Front of Aragón, while the rest came from the UGT, from leftist youth organizations, the ranks of the Communist Party, or other parties of the Popular Front. It was a heterogeneous mass of combatants, often difficult to control, which was left to useless excesses but that fought valiantly, despite being afflicted by inadequate armament and often left without heavy artillery, with means of transport Improvised or even non-existent. Enthusiasm and confidence in the revolution, after the defeat of the military uprising in Barcelona, Madrid, Valencia and other cities, generated some paradoxes, so many militiamen considered normal, especially in the first weeks of the war, to stop the struggle in order to take nap, or simply to go back home to sleep, leaving the front unprotected: the harsh reality of the war quickly wiped out all this. The total number of foreigners in the militia, that is to say, the ones which remained outside the International Brigades, is difficult to establish, but could hover between 3,000 and 4,500 volunteers, including a large number of women, sometimes deployed in first line, at least until October 30, 1936, when the government, through the edict "men on the front and women in the rear", decided to forbid their presence on the battlefront, assigning all the young women to health services, logistics or support.

▲This photo, taken in Barcelona in the autumn of 1936, shows a group of Hungarian volunteers. Most of them wear the isabelino cap with red wool tassel and cotton jumpsuits of various colours on civilian clothes, the typical uniform in the first months of the war. The insignia of the unit, mounted here in the manner of a banner, could be seen on a red background with yellow or white letters. The unit was named in honour to the Secretary of the Communist Party of Hungary in exile. Like many Eastern European volunteers, at the end of the Spanish Civil War, Hungarians faced a real odyssey, which for many of them ended tragically in Nazi concentration camps. (Author's archive)

COMMUNIST AND SOCIALIST INTERNATIONAL UNITS

The first major foreign unit of Communist inspiration was the Thaelmann Centuria, created in late August 1936 in Barcelona, and formed by German-speaking volunteers, and others from Sweden, Norway and Denmark. Since the beginning of September, the men of the Thaelmann fought in the Front of Aragón, in Huesca, Tardienta and Alcubierre, supported by an ingenious armoured truck of its own invention. In Aragón, the unit was framed in the Republican militia corps and received a number of names that make it difficult to identify: at the beginning of September it was the 31st Centuria, Maxim Gorki Battalion, 19 de July Column, later, it became the Thaelmann Centuria, 19 de July Batallion, Carlos Marx Column. On October 25, transferred to Albacete for instruction, the centuria was transformed into a battalion and joined the 9th Mobile Brigade, which gave origin to the XI International Brigade on November 11. The presence of foreigners in Spain increased considerably before the end of summer, despite the closing of the French border. Many of those who came from abroad had crossed the Pyrenees on foot, along one of the many mountain trails in the region. They were decided volunteers, since many were already in the condition of fugitives in France, Switzerland or Belgium, where there were associations and groups of residents of Germany, Italy and other nationalities, with many years of exile on their shoulders. The news from Spain represented for many the sign of recovery of the struggle and, for this reason, the first to arrive were those who had already left their country, especially those who possessed more than one reason to fight in Spain, especially after learning that the Rebels enjoyed military support from Germany and Italy. The first training of volunteers of the Communist Party of Italy in exile took place in Barcelona and left the city for the Front of Aragón the 30th August, where it was added to the other foreign formations within the Carlos Marx Column, who fought the enemy for the first time in the Huesca sector. At the end of August, another unit of Italian volunteers belonging to the Third International was formed, called the Gastone Sozzi Centuria, commanded by Angelo Antonini, and later, by Gottardo Rinaldi, with the Arditi del Popolo (The People's Brave Ones) Italian-Brazilian

▼ One of the rare images of the Giustizia e Libertà Battalion of the Francisco Ascaso Column of the CNT-FAI, on its arrival at the Front of Huesca, in August 1936. The unit, formed in Barcelona by Carlo Rosselli and Camillo Berneri, included Anarchists, Socialists, Republicans and other Italian Antifascists, formed under the command of Mario Angeloni. At the dawn of August 28, 1936, the battalion fought its first battle, repelling an enemy assault in the Monte Pelado sector. The trenches were still incomplete, but sheltered with huge piles of wheat and straw, along the Zaragoza-Huesca road. The Italians opened fire on the enemy advancing on the left flank. Commander Angeloni, who was sleeping next to the first machine gun, jumped up and ordered another machine gun to move to the left in order to defend the riflemen, and then took a bag full of grenades and headed to the front line, but fell immediately because of a shot coming form an armoured car on the road. The Italian volunteers fought boldly and, despite the improvised defences, managed to repel the attack, consisting of 700 men supported by machine guns, armoured vehicles and a battery of cannons. (Author's archive)

Francesco Leone as political commissar. Later, the unit became the 22nd Centuria of the Libertad Column, a formation of the popular militia of Catalonia, also known as the Partit Socialista Unificat de Catalunya.

On September 9, the centuria moved with the rest of the column to the Front of Madrid, where confronted Rebel troops in combat the following day in Real Cenicientos, during the defence of the Extremadura road. At the exact time of entering the line, the unit consisted of 86 Italians, 14 Frenchmen, 2 Belgians and 1 Dane, in addition to 2 Hungarians and 34 poles. Moreover, the latter included a section of machine guns with the name of Jaroslav Dabrowski Platoon. Among the French volunteers were professional soldiers, even of high rank, like Lieutenant Colonel Jules Vincent, who was put in the service by the Government of Madrid once the generals' uprising was known. Between 16 and 18 October, the men of the Sozzi Century fought hard in Chapinería, before being sent to the rearguard and, later, to Albacete, to the International Brigades' base, where the survivors formed the 3rd Company of the Garibaldi Battalion. The first groups of volunteers from Central Europe were also formed in the units of the PCE and the PSUC. At the beginning of September 1936, it was also formed the 38th Dimitrov Century in Catalonia within the Carlos Marx Column, in honour of the Secretary of the Komintern. It was formed by Bulgarian, Polish and Czech volunteers; while another unit, composed mainly of Hungarians, was added to the same column and assumed the name of Rakosi Group. This last contingent, established within the Catalan JSU, grouped some forty members of the dissolved Communist Party of Hungary, most of them from the USSR, where they had taken asylum since the 1920s. It was a vanguard of approximately 600 political emigrants of various nationalities that the Comintern sent to Spain to form the International Brigades, a very convenient way to get rid of their presence and infiltrate agents of the NKVD. Along with the private volunteers and secret agents, future international commanders came from the USSR, first class revolutionary fighters from the Frunze Military Academy, such as Manfred Stern (known as Emilio Kleber), Maté Zalka (Paul Lukacs), János Gálicz (General Gal), Wilhelm Zeisser (Gomez), Karol Świerczewski (Walter) and many more, as well as prominent members of the Italian Communist Party in exile, such as Palmiro Togliatti and Giancarlo Pajetta, destined to play important roles once the International Brigades were formed. Some of the militias mobilized by the PSUC in Catalonia, including those with foreign volunteers, came urgently to the Front of Madrid, where in early September participated in the struggle against the Rebels advancing towards the capital. In comparison with the clashes that occurred since then in Aragón, the surroundings of the capital were much more violent and the improvised militia units could hardly cope with the commanders' lack of preparation and the armament shortage, which consisted of old muskets confiscated in the Army arsenals and almost always heterogeneous. This resulted in the fact that, in a same unit, there were weapons of different calibre, with detrimental effects for the regulation of munitions. The first international volunteers fought mainly on the fronts of Aragón and Madrid, with the exception of some small units that received

the baptism of fire in the Basque Country, where they had arrived in mid-August to defend Irun. This population represented the only access on the Northwest border that remained loyal to the Republic and it was expected that weapons and supplies could be obtained from the neighbouring France. The militia formations present in the sector were led by the French Socialist Jacques Menachem, former captain of the Army. In total, the foreigners amounted to some sixty volunteers of about ten different nationalities: the Valery Wroblesky Group, commanded by the Polish Communist Francisco Palka, included 9 men, the Edgar André Group, formed by ten Germans, including its leader, a Communist known by the war name of "Papá" (Dad); a dozen Italians gathered in the Gorizia Group, led by the Communist Remigio Maurovich of Istria, an old acquaintance of the Fascist political police; and, finally, a small group run by a veteran of the Légion étrangère, a French native of Bohemia, along with a Jew named Bessarabia Leib Jampolski, then political commissar at the XI International Brigade, consisting of three German volunteers, a Polish, a Frenchman and a Belgian. Other foreign volunteers, including some Spaniards residing in France, were part of Basque units and local parties' militias. The contingent was politically composed: the militiamen were mostly Anarchists, Catalan Communists, and Basque Separatists. Apart from the leaders, very few could boast of having some combat experience. Among the foreign volunteers were mechanics, drivers, sailors, and students. The age of the combatants was very varied, there was even a father with his son: the French Louis and Henry Brion. The armament provided was quite varied and probably not enough for everyone. In fact, the militant Attilio Galeazzi, deployed as a "bomb launcher", does not go unnoticed among the defenders. Many Italian volunteers were long-term expatriates in neighbouring France and some had combat experience, such as the Anarchist Alessio Donati, an artillery officer during the Great War. Subjected to the air bombings and the Rebel artillery, the defenders suffered heavy losses without being able to return the attack, while the opponents proceeded to conquer Mount Picoqueta, advancing towards the town of San Marcial, to the north of Irun. The opponents sought to remove the control of the routes of communication with France and Catalonia, so, on September 3, they were about to conquer the bridge of Hendaye, which joined Irun to the border. Around this strategic objective the fight intensified, which continued until the afternoon of 4 September, when the militia units were forced to fall back due to lack of ammunition. The Italians Maurovich and Donati fell on the bridge of Hendaye, through which a large number of civilians had just passed through France. Another Italian named Arrigo Gojak, who had been wounded in the battle, was assassinated the following day by the Rebels at the Irún hospital. A German Antifascist, called Stern, died in a French hospital, while the volunteer Giovanni Battista Frati, wounded in combat, received first aid in the French Gendarmerie infirmary. Many militiamen took shelter on the other side of the boundary and crossed the border, showing their empty cartridges to the French guards. During the episode, six Italian volunteers lost their lives in the struggle around Irun.

ANARCHIST INTERNATIONAL UNITS

In the 1930s, a considerable part of the Spanish population was adhered or sympathized with a libertarian ideology, which in turn could have a very efficient trade union organization. In the bastions of Catalonia and Aragón, these brought together almost half of the workers registered in all trade unions. Under the initials of FAI (Federación Anarquista Ibérica, Iberian Anarchist Federation) and CNT (Confederación Nacional de Trabajadores, National Confederation of Labour), cultural circles and associations were in contact with libertarian organizations abroad, but, unlike the Comintern, Anarchists never established centres to recruit foreign volunteers or to ease their participation or arrival into Spain. The only exception was the French section of the CNT of Puigcerdà, a city located on the eastern border of the Pyrenees, in Spanish territory. The city is less than one kilometre from the French border and was elected in July 1936 as a base for the Pyrenees propaganda office, in order to strengthen cooperation between the Anarchists of the two neighbouring countries. As of March 1937, the Section also began to fulfil the role of Auxiliary Transit Centre for the Anarchist volunteers who were heading to Catalonia. The Section, with a thousand difficulties, remained active until May 1937, when it closed its doors due to the lack of funds and the frustration caused by the riots in Barcelona.

The influx of volunteers in the confederal militia was carried out in the most diverse way. In the wave of the spontaneity of the militants, however, a real trend of recruitment was experienced during the summer of 1936. As expected, the first to come were the French, and with them, the Italian Anarchists exiled in France, who rushed to fight the insurgents, proving to be very active in supplying the first units nationwide. The Italian Fascist police took note in those weeks of many clandestine expeditions that had as protagonists Anarchists who during time had been under close vigilance, and that, with singular recklessness, arrived in Spain by the most diverse ways. Adriano Ferrari, Renzo de Peretti, and Enzo Costantini, the three Italian Anarchists murdered in Barcelona by the guardias de asalto (assault guards) during the days of May 1937, had joined the CNT militia in January after defecting from a unit of Mussolini's Corpo Truppe Volontarie. The way travelled by the "subversives" Calamassi, Cocco and Guerrieri, of the Francisco Ascaso Confederal Column was longer, but less risky, as they left for Chambery, crossing the Alpine passes afoot, and, from there, they travelled to Marseilles to sail with destination Barcelona. The rejection to the discipline and traditional models of the "bourgeois" armies led to the adoption of a completely new terminology in the militia to refer to the functions and units, even if in some cases they were only slight differences. The organisational structure of the CNT-FAI columns also influenced the other militias, including those of the Catalan POUM, a staunchly Antistalinist party and the Anarchists' main ally. At the base of the militia were the assemblies, where all the decisions were taken through the principle of direct democracy, thus abolishing the traditional military hierarchy.

The smallest military unit was the group or platoon of 25 militiamen, under the orders of a delegate elected by the Assembly, but revocable at any time. Four or more groups formed a centuria, guided in the same style by an official delegate. Therefore, four or five centurias constituted a group or battalion. Finally, a minimum of two battalions gave birth to a column. Although the highest positions were undoubtedly in keeping with the mandate of the Assembly, in the CNT-FAI militia, however, there was a permanent High Staff, where militiamen with specific military knowledge accessed the Technical-Military Council, immediately subordinated to the War Committee, the body of political-military management of the columns. Even in the highest echelons, ranks remained elective, but once hierarchies were established, self-discipline required the militia to obey orders, at least until the next assembly. In the famous Durruti Column, led by the eminent and respected union leader who gave name to the unit, a commander delegated by the international volunteers, the Frenchman Louis Berthomieux, took a seat in the Technical Council.

Thanks to David Berry's research, while investigating the archives of the CNT-FAI, it has been possible to obtain a broader view of French participation within the ranks of the Anarchist militias and, secondly, the international presence in the same units from July 1936. On the basis of 332 names of French Anarchists who were in Spain in various extents, presumably before May 1937, 225 occupied positions of combatants in the confederal militia. The lists also include names of Italians, Germans, Swiss, Bulgarians, Russians, Czechs, Portuguese, Belgians, Dutch and others of indeterminate nationality. According to the author himself, this list is far from complete and, above all, does not consider volunteers with Catalan, Spanish, and Basque surnames that could be of French origin, or from some country in South America. Several French volunteers, i.e. 157, circulated within the Durruti Column, while 37 other foreigners, mostly French, merged in the Ortiz Column before December 1936, bringing together 10 French volunteers at the end of July. Another 10 French appear in the Los Aguiluchos Column, 5 in the Libertad Column and one in each Spanish column, Hilario Zamora, García Oliver, and Aviatores; all deployed in the Front of Aragón, except the Libertad Column, assigned to the defence of Madrid. According to the same source, 19 French militiamen also took arms in the Italian section of Ascaso Column. In the same column, the Eric Müsham Group, which included volunteers from Germany and Switzerland, was formed on 25 July 1936. At the end of August, the French and Italian volunteers of the Durruti Column joined to form a group of about fifty men, which took the name of Sébastien Faure Group, in honour to a libertarian pedagogue from Saint-Étienne, and went on to form the first International Anarchist centuria. Together with the Anarchist movement, the first Italian Antifascist organizations that incited their members from abroad to intervene in Spain were Giustizia e Libertà, the Maximalist Socialist Party, the Bordigist minority of the Communist Party, and the Republican Party. With them, some reformist Communists and Socialists also agreed to interfere, contrary to the instructions of waiting of the Communist and Socialist Party, which, according to the indications of the respective International, invited their members to collect funds, food, and medicine for the Spanish Republic, but not to support it with weapons. The inclusion of volunteers within these militias was not always regulated by political affiliation, and, in the case of Italian Antifascists, there

ITALIAN VOLUNTEERS

Thanks to the work of the Association of Voluntary Anti-Fascist Combatants in Spain, it is possible to examine a sample of 140 volunteers, from which we can reconstruct a sufficiently detailed biography, going back in many of them to the date and place of birth, the profession, and other useful elements to form a large enough statistical framework. In the sample there is also a woman, the Milanese anarchist Angelica Astolfi, present in Barcelona in 1938. One volunteer is originally from Rhodes, with an unequivocal Greek name and surname, but resides in Imperia. Two other volunteers come from Switzerland and could be Italian-speaking Swiss citizens.

Expatriates abroad before 1936:	Emigrated before 1921, or children of emigrants:	Escaped from Italy after 1936:	Uncertain:
47,2%	28,9%	16,7%	7,2%

Profession:

Workers	Artisans	Peasants	Commerce	Transport	Militars	Teachers	Other*	Unknown
31,6%	17,9%	7,3%	6,3%	6,3%	2,1%	2,1%	2,7%	23,7%

* 1 lawyer, 1 actor, 1 insurer, 1 publicist, 1 editor

Note: among the military there are two non-commissioned officers and a lieutenant colonel, Paolo Avogadro, from Novara, expelled from the Regio Esercito after the discovery of his affiliation with Giustizia e Libertà and expatriated clandestinely in 1938.

Age:

Under 21	From 22 to 30	Over 31	Over 40	Over 50	Unknown
2,8%	26,9%	46,8%	11,4%	4,2%	7,9%

are numerous examples of coexistence among volunteers of different ideologies. The first proposal to form a militia to which all Italian Antifascists could have access without regard to ideology is attributed to the Anarchist Camillo Berneri. The opportunity was exploited by other Antifascist exiles, and an agreement was reached in which non-Anarchists could enter a column sponsored by the CNT, and in turn these would renounce to give the unit a specific ideological sphere. On 5 August 1936, an agreement was reached with the other parties: 'Italian Anarchists enrolled in the C.N.T. and F.A.I. militia -according to the agenda of the meeting- fraternally greet the Italian Antifascist volunteers of Giustizia e Libertà, the Maximalist Socialist Party, the Republican Action and the Republican Socialist Party, which have preferred, recognizing the important role of Anarchism in Spain in the struggle against Fascism, our formation instead of any other militia'. A Coordination Committee was later established with the task of verifying and making better use of the technical and military knowledge of the various members of the newly formed militia. About 130 Italian volunteers joined the ranks of the Francisco Ascaso Column, formed in Barcelona in August 1936 by Catalan and Aragonese Anarchists. The Italians led by Carlo Rosselli joined Berneri's proposal and met in a section known as the Giustizia e Libertà Column, structured in a half-company of riflemen and one of machine guns. The reception of so many volunteers not aligned with the positions of the Anarchists in the units of the CNT-FAI testifies, on the one hand, the supremacy of these formations in the Antifascist field and, on the other, a way of catalysing the presence of foreign volunteers in their own militia, in order to counteract the Communists 's similar initiatives, especially those linked to the Comintern. It was probably presented in this way a proposal by a representative of the CNT of Barcelona in an assembly of early August 1936, in order to avoid the influx of foreigners, motivating the assumption to keep the revolutionary movement in a native dimension. Indeed, the Assembly decided to support the Anarchist militiamen with the Catalan border guards for some time, in order to intensify the border controls. But, before the end of summer, various volunteers from different backgrounds already participated in the fighting around Aragón framed in the most important foreign formation among those of the CNT-FAI, the International Group of the Durruti Column. At the beginning of November, a part of this column, which already had a total of almost 7,000 combatants, went to Madrid with Buenaventura Durruti himself, while in Aragón, in the sector of Belchite, another great confederal unit remained, the Ortiz Column, which in December 1936 included dozens of internationals. Despite initial hostility to foreign presence, all Anarchist formations, including volunteers from abroad, were immediately sent to the front of battle. The Ascaso Column arrived in Aragón in mid-August 1936, including the Italian section under the orders of Carlo Rosselli and the Peruvian Republican Mario Angeloni, Italian expatriates in 1932. The Bolognese Anarchist Vindice Rabitti was appointed to the rank of "political leader". Of the two commanders, Rosselli had very little military experience, but was the most gifted as a leader. Angeloni, with brilliant personality, seemed able to establish direct contact with the militia, but, despite having been in the Army, tended to neglect the discipline of his men.

The section came to the front with 150 combatants. The heavy armament consisted of four machine guns; the ammunition and equipment had been transported on the back of a mule. Together with other militias involved in the fight in the Front of Aragón, the Ascaso column received the baptism of fire at dawn on August 28, when it rejected an assault on the Monte Pelado, a prominence of the Galocha plateau, located between the Aragonese cities of Huesca and Almudévar. The attackers were supported by a cannon and some armoured vehicles, but the militia defended stubbornly and, after four hours of fighting, repelled the Rebels, albeit with many casualties, including Commander Mario Angeloni, who died along with other seven Italian volunteers from his unit. The section command went to Giuseppe Bifolchi, who had already been an NCO during the First World War. The other foreign militiamen present in the columns of the CNT participated together with their

▲ Emilio Canzi and Giuseppe Mioli, volunteers in the Francisco Ascaso Column. Emilio Canzi (left), later, leader of a brigade of the 26th Division (former Ascaso Column), had been sergeant of snipers in the First World War and, later, organizer of the Arditi del Popolo in Piacenza. Expatriated in late 1928, he left for Spain with the news of the military coup to enlist in the CNT-FAI militia. Afflicted, like many other Italian Anarchists, by the events of the Republican policy, the "Anarchist Colonel" abandoned the fight, but, after September 8, 1943, he was one of the main leaders of the Antifascist resistance in the area of Piacenza. Canzi died in a car accident in November 1945, after donating all his belongings to the hospital staff he had been admitted in. Canzi and Mioli wear the typical suit of coarse cotton, sand or light brown colour, and the belts and holster of a local Astra pistol in brown leather. The black beret had no distinctives and often replaced the common red and black isabelino side cap among the CNT-FAI militiamen.

Catalan and Aragonese comrades at the Battle of Pina de Ebro, on October 16, 1936, which ended with an expensive victory for the Republicans. In the clash, probably the most violent at the date, 80 foreign volunteers lost their lives.

In the other sector of the Front of Aragón, at the end of the Nationalist offensive in Perdiguera of October 1936, the international Group of the Durruti Column had lost 170 men in battle of the 240 deployed at the beginning of the offensive. Like other Anarchist units, the international group was considered an assault unit and as such was employed in the battle, accumulating a tragic record of loss in combat, culminating in the tragic action of October 22 at the Battle of Perdiguera, when 37 foreign volunteers remained isolated from the rest of the unit. Surrounded and without hope of receiving help, they fell one after another without giving up, among them the young August Marx, a German volunteer of only nineteen years. Already turned into soldiers of the International Company of the 26th Division of the Popular Army, in early April 1937, the foreign volunteers of the column had about 130 men. On April 7, the company was deployed in battle and launched to the attack of the Hermitage of Santa Quiteria, a strategically and important position in the Tardienta sector, where even in the preceding autumn fierce clashes costed many losses to the Republican militia. Despite an initial success, this time, thanks to the support of a large number of artillery and mortar pieces, the Republicans failed to isolate their opponents because of a lack of coordination between the forces and were forced to retire. The International Company lost 16 men in the battle, another 4 disappeared, and 23 were wounded. In the battle, several young nurses also lost their lives. Of all the formations in the Popular Militia, the Anarchists registered a high percentage of women, who remained with the militias even after the edict of October 1936. Everything tends to indicate that the largest number of foreign volunteers of the CNT-FAI were of French nationality, with at least 17 women within the 259 volunteers identified, and that most were in the Durruti Column. One of them, Emilienne Morin, served as coordinator of the technical services of the column on the Front of Aragón until December 1936. Although they worked as nurses or in other tasks in the rear, some young women paid their part in the struggle with their own lives. In September, the French Susanne Hans, aged 22, fell during an assault on Ferlete, while the following month the nurses Georgette Kokoczinski and Juliette Baudard remained victims of the fighting in Perdiguera. During the Francoist offensive in this sector, the International Group also lost its general delegate, former French artillery captain Louis Berthomieux, replaced on 16 October by the Parisian officer Roger Boutefeu from the Jeunesses Anarchistes-Communistes (Anarchist-Communist

▼ Parade by a group of members of the Battalion de la Muerte (Death Battalion), one of the international formations established in Catalonia after the military coup, on March 14, 1937 in Barcelona. The battalion was formed around a group of Italian Anarchists exiled in Catalonia, who were joined by other Italians from France and South America. In February 1937, the leader of the unit, the Italian-Argentinian Candido Testa, managed to obtain the necessary funds from the Catalan government to equip his men in view of the parade that took place in the presence of the president of the Generalitat, Lluís Companys. The unit wore a grey-coloured jacket on a black turtleneck sweater, loose or tied grey trousers, and a dark leather belt. The dagger of his belt was probably inspired by that of the Italian Arditi of the Great War, but the black beret embroidered with a skull and the overall appearance of the uniform seemed a clumsy imitation of Mussolini's Fascist uniforms. This attracted criticism by many of the present. In other photos of this parade women dressed in the same uniform can be seen, but their presence in the battalion must have occurred only during the parade.

Youth), alias Coudry, aged 25. He, together with the Algerian Anarchist Mohamed Saïl, was later accused of desertion, after being wounded and hospitalised in Barcelona, from where they would both return to France in January 1937.

The climate of suspicion and political hatred existing in the Army of Aragón High Staff generated the rumour that Coudry had deliberately wounded himself to return home. Because of this suspicion, he had to defend himself back to his homeland. Although the cases of desertion were quite rare, the mobility of foreign volunteers within the militias of the CNT-FAI makes it difficult to form a general framework, leaving us with a fragmentary reconstruction of reality. One of the most important actions in the Front of Aragón in which an international militia participated was the assault on Huesca, which took place between 6 and 7 April 1937, when the Italian section of the Ascaso Column tried, together with the militiamen of the POUM, to conquer the fortified site of Carrascal. In this action a department made from fire fighters was deployed, trained by the Anarchist Abruzzese Antonio Closei, who personally directed the action, but was deadly wounded. Within the Anarchist militia, the most known, and at the same time controversial foreign unit, was the Malatesta Centuria, constituted in Barcelona a few days after the military uprising, on the initiative of the Italian resident Nicola Menna.

The unit increased its ranks with the entry of Italian Anarchists who lived in Catalonia and others who rushed to the news of the military rebellion. In September, the unit changed its name to the grotesque title of Battalion de la Muerte (Death Battalion), choosing as a symbol the skull and crossbones, and deploying three companies plus a section of "staff", framed, as other international units, in the Ascaso Column. The members of the battalion gathered to train on a farm near Sant Adrià de Besòs, with weapons provided by the economic adviser of the Generalitat of Catalonia, Diego Abad de Santillán. Information about this unit is sometimes contradictory or becomes reticent about some important details. Some of the authors who treated the militias of the CNT-FAI never mention the battalion, while other sources speak of it in a very positive way, or in a totally negative, referring to anecdotes little flattering. In mid-September 1936, the battalion first faced against the Rebels with nothing but unsatisfactory results. In the memoirs of the Italian volunteer Francesco Scotti, collected by Davide Lajolo, a mention is made about a battalion of Italian Anarchists recently arrived at the Front of Aragón, in the sector of Huesca: 'I had barely left the front line with my column, when a strange unit called the Death Battalion reached the front. They were quarrelsome and frantic Anarchists; they came from Barcelona and moved to our front to conquer Huesca. Angry at our advice of prudence, they brutally told us they would teach us how to make war. They went out with their trucks to the entrenched bastion of Huesca. They unleashed a hurricane of fire but did not spend many hours in the trucks and returned to the rear.' Following the failure of the Huesca confrontation, the battalion was sent to reorganize at the base of Santa Perpètua de Mogoda and went under the orders of the Italian-Argentinian Anarchist Candido Testa, also known as Mario Weber. It is not clear to whom the new commander would have replaced at the front of the battalion, which, according to some, had been directed by Camillo Berneri until then, although it is true that him, afflicted by sight problems, was no longer on the front in mid-September. The men of the Death Battalion, however, were seen in the parade of March 14, 1937 in Barcelona, arousing contradictory impressions, especially by the grim uniform they had adopted, judged too similar to the Camicie Nere (Blackshirts). Despite the libertarian fervour and aura of romantic dedication to the revolutionary cause surrounding its components, the unit's reputation remained ambiguous. The Italian exiles' press in Argentina described the battalion with enthusiastic tones, illustrating the actions of the commander and those of his subordinates, such as Emilio Strapellini, head of the second company: 'From Rovereto, Trentino, and former captain of the Alpini, former secretary of the League of Human Rights in Paris, [he] was detained for 54 months on the island of Lipari. [...] Both Testa and Strapellini, through funny faces, do not deny the steel temper of the Italian combatants'.

Other witnesses, on the other hand, did not show the same enthusiasm and admiration: a few days before, a volunteer adhered to Giustizia e Libertà had written to a director of the organization that he distrusted Testa, calling him 'a thief', and, about the Death Battalion, that 'no one took it seriously'. Equally ambiguous is still the question

Foreign volunteers in CNT-FAI units from August 1936 to January 1937

Aragón	French	Italians	Germans	Swiss	Other
Columna Durruti Grupo Internacional	151	65	120	12	65
Columna Ascaso:	25	240	29	5	52
Columna Ortiz:	16	18	10		19
Columna Los Aguiluchos:	7		40	3	2
Columna de Hierro:	2		3		6
Columna Aviatores:	2				
Columna Españole:	1				1
Columna Garcia Oliver:	1	2			
Columna Hilario Zamora:	1				2
Madrid					
Columna Libertad:	5				1
Columna Del Rosal (including Bateria Sacco and Vanzetti):	1	30	10	2	

Taken from Berry; Nelles; Enzensberger, Alpert and others.

▲ In the Front of Huesca, in Aragón, the columns of the CNT-FAI gathered most of the international units, such as the Giustizia e Libertà and De la Muerte battalions within the Ascaso Column, and the Eric Müsham Group, formed by German Anarchists, in the Los Aguiluchos Column. In October 1936, this formation used a red and black flag with a three-pointed star and a yellow inscription.

of who were the commanders that took turns to lead the unit. Following a new disaster, suffered in the assault on an enemy station in Santa Desastre, near Tardienta, in April 1937, the Staff was convinced that it was necessary to entrust the battalion to an expert officer, chosen from a list of candidates, including Francesco Fausto Nitti, nephew of the Italian statesman Francesco Saverio Nitti, former fighter of the First World War and adhered to Giustizia e Libertà. However, Nitti, which other authors place at the head of the Rojo y Negro Battalion, another unit of the CNT-FAI, never mention the unity that he led, making all its history not clear. Even the dates relating to the appointment of the commanders do not coincide, if we consider that Candido Testa, still on the head of the battalion, was convalescent in Barcelona in mid-June, due to a wound received in Huesca. On the other hand, official documents also increase uncertainty. A report on the state of the force of the CLIII Mixed Brigade, from November 27, 1937, certifies that Nitti was in charge of the 3rd Battalion of the brigade and, if the latter had commanded the Death Battalion from May 19 to July 15, 1937, it can be deduced that the unit had become, once reorganized by Nitti, in one of the brigade's battalions. Assuming, however, that Nitti was aware of the events of the unit, and according to the reputation of Candido Testa, it is equally probable that he preferred to remain silent on the matter, hastening to accept his appointment as commander of an artillery battery of the CXL Brigade. On the other hand, in the memoirs of the Commander-in-chief of the Army of Aragón, Vicente Guarner, several foreign units are mentioned within the formations of the militias, in particular the Giustizia e Libertà Centuria and the Death Batallion, and in the same reports, it is referred to a non-conclusive offensive action conducted by the battalion in Almudévar. Guarner later recalled the transfer of all militiamen who could still fight the Montalbán sector, in the area of Calamocha, where they were involved in a series of clashes, which ended alternately and where they always suffered many losses.

At the end of the summer of 1937, the battalion had dissolved, and most of its members had returned to France, while a party had agreed to move to the XII International Brigade. Instead, according to Carlos Engel, author of the Historia de las Brigades Mixtas en el Ejército Popular, in May 1937, the battalion was framed in the CXLII Mixed Brigade, together with a Basque battalion and another Spanish. The Italian Alessandro Contini was elected to the head of the unit. Later, in the next October, the entire brigade was dissolved, and all the men joined the 32nd Division. A significant German presence has been recorded within the CNT-FAI militia, thanks to the work of Dieter Nelles, who examined the biography of at least 250 of his countrymen who, for various reasons, worked with Anarchist organizations, both as combatants, propagandists, journalists, or collaborators in various fields. Although in his country Syndicalism had not a large political reality, it was still very active during the years of exile. Gathered at the DAS (Gruppe Deutsche Anarcho-Syndikalisten im Ausland, German Anarcho-syndicalist Group Abroad), German libertarians were naturally attracted to the prestige of the Spanish movement and, in turn, acted as a point of aggregation for other Anarchists in central and northern Europe. The first unit of volunteers of the DAS was formed on August 27, 1936 in the Los Aguiluchos Column, and took the name of Erich Müsham Group. Together with his Spanish comrades, the Germans fought in Aragón, where they received the baptism of fire in the Huesca cemetery in early September. Other German Anarchists have been identified in different CNT units, such as 29 volunteers who arrived from Germany and recalled in their letters the Social Democrat Otto Albrecht in the Ascaso Column. Another 12 could be found in the Ortiz Column, as well as individual presences of officers, as in the case of a battalion of the Rosales Column in Madrid, commanded by the Social Democrat Carl Oster. Between October and November 1936, most of the foreign volunteers present in the CNT-FAI militia in Aragón met in the international Group of the Durruti Column. It is estimated that about 150 German volunteers were militarized in this unit, although in the front they never coincided more than a hundred at the same time. As with the Italian volunteers, even the Germans joined the federal militia without taking into account its ideology of origin, although among the German Antifascists the rivalry with the Marxists was very energetic, for obvious reasons. Also, in the Front of Aragón, within the CNT-FAI militia, an international artillery battery was installed, called Sacco y Vanzetti Battery, before the end of the summer of 1936, commanded during a certain period by the French Anarchosyndicalist Paul Chacon, under the war name of Máximo Mas. The unit was made up of Italian volunteers, a dozen Germans, and some more of different nationalities. As an assistant and military adviser, the Communist dissident Ernst Günther, a former officer of the German Army, worked until 1937. The battery was part of the Tierra y Libertad Column, considered one of the units chosen from the Catalan CNT-FAI, and was sent to the Madrid front in late September where it participated in the defence of the city. Then, during the following April, it was framed in the CLIII Brigade, with which it fought again in Aragón, in the sectors of Teruel and Cuenca.

A precise reconstruction carried out in the archives of the FAI-CNT would indicate that at least 1,500 international volunteers were present in the Anarchist units between July 1936 and April 1937, until the confederal militia was definitely classified inside the Republican Army. In this new context, the isolated careers of foreign commanders stand out, such as the "Anarchist Colonel" Emilio Canzi, future partisan leader, head of a brigade of the 26th Division until June 1937.

From this date, it is almost impossible to determine the foreign presence in the Ejército Popular (Republican Popular Army), taking into account that many

▲ Under the black and red flags of the CNT-FAI, the foreign volunteers of the Durruti Column advance behind their banner, during a parade in Barcelona in October 1936. While in the Ascaso Column many of the internationals came from Italy, in the Durruti the French presence dominated the total number of combatants. (Author's archive)

left Spain under the threat of repression unleashed by the government of Negrín after the events in Barcelona. This wave of blind and senseless repressive fury overwhelmed one of the main defenders of international participation in the Civil War, the Italian Camillo Berneri, shot in Barcelona on May 5, 1937 together with his main collaborator, Francesco Barbieri. The Italian presence in the confederal militia must be regarded as one of the most numerous and recognized with more than 500 volunteers, followed by the French, with more than 300, and by the Germans, with 250. Other Anarchist volunteers entered Spain individually or together within more or less organized groups from Switzerland, Russia, Ukraine, Belarus, Argentina, Poland, Hungary, Bulgaria, Scandinavia, the United States, and Great Britain.

POUM INTERNATIONAL UNITS

Andreu Nin, a Catalan Communist, for a few months, personal secretary of Leon Trotsky, was the charismatic leader of the POUM (Partido Obrero de Unificación Marxista, Workers' Party of Marxist Unification), a political formation within the galaxy of Communist dissents against Stalin in Spain. Although Trotsky himself had unauthorized the work of Nin's party from Mexico City, many foreign volunteers who did not support Moscow's awaiting policy merged with the POUM militia, which then hosted not only the members of the Fourth International, but all the diverse Marxist-inspired revolutionary dissident parties.

The POUM was based in Lleida, but later moved to Barcelona, during the creation of the Central Committee of Antifascist Militias in the same city, which was also joined by the CNT-FAI. In August 1936, the POUM militia staff credited the first foreign volunteers to form the Lenin International Column, which, in mid-September, included a total of between 250 and 300 militiamen of various nationalities, gathered in a "clash battalion" run by German officers. Among these volunteers were the approximately 180 combatants of the French Gauche Revolutionnaire Socialiste (Revolutionary Socialist Left) and the left wing of the Belgian Workers' Party; less numerous, but well represented, the Italian group gathered the militants of the Maximist Socialist Party and the Bordigist left wing of the Communist Party. The Lenin Column also grouped some English from the Independent Labour Party, including one of the most famous volunteers on the other side of the channel, writer George Orwell, who spent 18 months in Spain and left testimony of the events of the war in the book Homage to Catalonia. The column worked together with the other units of the POUM in Aragón, participating in the fight in the sector of Huesca, until the assault on the trenches of Carrascal in April 1937. At that time, the Lenin Column became the 29th Division of the Republican Popular Army, including volunteers from at least a dozen nationalities, mostly Italian, German, British, and French. According to recent surveys conducted by Andy Durgan, at least 700 foreign volunteers, including many women, worked in the POUM militia. In the international column he worked until October 1936, with the rank of captain of the motorised section, the Argentinean Communist Michèle Feldman, also known as Mika, partner of the volunteer French-Argentinian Hyppolite Etchebéhère, who fell in Sigüenza in August 1936. The section, described in the reports by Feldmann himself, included "two trucks, three cars, one hundred men and a gearless machine gun proudly placed on one of the trucks."

▲ Francisco Ascaso, Buenaventura Durruti, Gregorio Jover. Three leaders of the Spanish anarchist movement FAI, CNT. in Paris in 1927.

Feldman, like other young people until October 1936, had raised in arms against the Rebels, earning the esteem of the other militia and a reputation as a woman of a steel character, so much so that, at the death of Etchebéhère, she was appointed head of the unit.

Mika led his unit on the Front of Madrid, in the Moncloa sector, where the POUM had established a battalion, becoming a true revolutionary legend and probably the only foreign woman to have a leadership role in a first line unit of the Popular Militia. Among the foreigners who played major roles within the Poumist militia, the most important was the Belgian Georges Kopp, an engineer and former army officer, who became commander of a regiment of the 29th Division, very popular in the militia for his singular and dangerous disdain shown in battle. After the events of May in Barcelona, by instigation of the PCE and the Soviet secret services, the POUM was declared illegal and all its structures were dissolved by force at the beginning of June 1937. Since that time, many of the foreigners of the Lenin column had to hurry to save the life and to avoid the imprisonment or the firing squad. Only a small part, most German-speaking, entered the International Brigades.

▲ A group of foreign volunteers of the Lenin Column, belonging to the Workers' Party of Marxist Unification (POUM), in the Front of Aragón in the autumn of 1936 around a French 7mm Hotchkiss machine gun. In the centre of the image, the most outstanding volunteer is the English writer George Orwell. According to recent research, there were at least 700 militarized foreigners in the POUM militia until June 1937, when the Trotskyist-inspired political organization was outlawed by Juan Negrín's Government. An analysis carried out on a database collected by Andy Durgan, historical consultant of director Ken Loach for the film Land and Freedom, which contains the biography of 150 foreign volunteers, men and women, shows the Italian contingent as predominant, followed by the British Independent Labour Party and by German, French, Belgian, and Swiss in prevalence. Other volunteers came from Algeria, Argentina, Austria, Australia, Brazil, Czechoslovakia, Cuba, Denmark, Ireland, the Netherlands, Peru, Portugal, Poland, Romania, and the United States. (Author's archive)

EPILOGUE

The Republican Government's decision of 30 September 1936, which transferred all the militia formations to a unified command, caused much discontent among the members of the formations that had occurred spontaneously in the wake of the uprising. Many of the Anarchist and POUM militiamen, openly antimilitarists, reluctantly resisted the idea of entering an army and submitting to orders of officers imposed from above. When political confrontation increased in intensity within the Antifascist side, other misunderstandings appeared. Within the CNT formations the debate became incandescent and came to involve the leaders of the movement, as the same Buenaventura Durruti and the "Colonel Delegate" Cipriano Miera, favourable, for various reasons, to form a military structure capable of keeping alive the fight and achieving the victory. In addition, the modest results obtained by the militia and the high rate of losses suffered in combat required a different operating guide. In many places, it was emphasized how the incompetence and irresponsibility of the commanders had caused genuine disasters, causing the loss of many human lives, especially in the Front of Aragón, in an unfinished wave of operations that caused the dramatic weakening of the enthusiasm of the assembled volunteers in arms, therefore being criticized. Although the Front of Aragón had stabilized, the militia had been unable not only to achieve the objective of which it was responsible, the reconquest of Zaragoza, but, also, smaller cities, such as Teruel and Huesca, were still in the hands of the enemy.

The variable course of the war on the different fronts produced a different view on what army to form. The controversy over the militarization of the militias was rising in tone in the Levante (the eastern Iberian coastal region of Spain), whereas, in the central front around Madrid, the hardness of the clashes had convinced even the most refractory on the need to introduce the methods and discipline of the regular troops. As Michael Alpert wrote in The Republican Army in the Civil War, compared to the militia in Aragón, those in Madrid were seen as hardened veterans, who accepted these changes with less hysteria. The defence of Madrid represented the first victory of the Republican forces. After this test, militia leaders had a clearer idea of the situation and could become aware of their military capabilities. However, even in Madrid the Popular Militia paid the triumph with the loss of important leaders, including the loss of Buenaventura Durruti, which was probably the one destined to weigh more on the overall balance on the Republican front.

▶ Vincenzo Tonelli (1916-2009), until a few years ago, the last garibaldino of the Spanish Civil War, with the new khaki uniform delivered to the International Brigades in the spring of 1937, consisting of a short jacket and wide trousers that stopped at the ankles. It is worth noting the alpargata style shoes, often used by the combatants on both sides to protect the boots from the unyielding lands of the Peninsula. (Kind courtesy of the AICVAS)

> **FORMATION OF AN INFANTRY BATTALION OF THE PEOPLE'S ARMY (OCTOBER 30, 1936)**
>
> **- Battalion:**
> Senior and assistant
> Transmissions Section
> 1st Fusiliers Company
> 2nd Fusiliers Company
> 3rd Fusiliers Company
> Fusiliers Company in reserve
> Machine gun Company
> Mortar Section (4 pieces)
>
> **- Fusiliers Company:**
> Captain
> 1st Section (with 1 mortar after November 1937)
> 2nd Section
> 3rd Section
> **- Section:**
> Lieutenant or Ensign
> 1st Platoon
> 2nd Platoon
>
> **- Platoon:**
> Sergeant
> 1st Equipment (6 riflemen)
> 2nd Equipment (4 riflemen, 1 machine gunner, 1 carrier)
> 3rd Equipment (6 riflemen)
>
> Each rifleman was equipped with a rifle and six grenades. The machine gun and the ammunition carrier were each armed with one gun. Each soldier was also equipped with a shovel.

Even among foreign volunteers, the loss of important leaders forced laments, such as the political commissioner of the Thaelmann Battalion, Hans Beimler, who fell in the Spanish capital at the end of December 1936; a character capable of mediating between the different tendencies and fomenting the dialogue during the Antifascist mealtimes.

The storming confrontation over the mobilization of the militia also had repercussions among the foreign volunteers, since, between January and March of 1937, almost all the French and Italians were presented at the International Company of the recently formed 26th Division (formerly, Durruti Column), abandoned as a sign of protest against the formation, while another 20 foreigners asked to join the International Brigade. In April 1937, the international column company consisted only of two-thirds of Germans and Swiss. Those who decided to stay, nevertheless, demanded to abolish the military greeting, to establish the same salary for soldiers and officers, freedom of press and discussion, and the creation of new councils run by the soldiers. The official militarization of the militia continued to be a serious problem, tolerated by the majority in the expectation of new military laws. However, it is estimated that at least a thousand militiamen left the Front of Aragón before April 1937, as a sign of protest towards the possibilist orientation of the CNT. The increase in repulsion towards the Army contributed to the growing influence of the Communists, considerably higher since Soviet aid arrived in Spain, while, to the Anarchist militants, together with other political forces not related to the Communist International, liked it little, if not, nothing.

As the American volunteer Bill Wood of the Durruti Column bitterly noticed in the spring of 1937, the CNT seemed to have lost all influence over the Popular Army. Anarchists were accused of blind and brutal anti-clerical violence and of having presented personal and ideological interests, that is, to carry forward the Revolution rather than the common cause of war, and to continue to reject the military framework; Ultimately to benefit the enemy even with accusations of intelligence.

The violence set in motion by some uncontrollable units had undoubtedly harmed the CNT-FAI, but the horrors of the Civil War and the ruthless destruction of the enemy were not exclusive to the Anarchists, who, along with the other political forces, had fought hard from the first moment. The propaganda of the parties linked to the CPSU raised the fight against the most radical political formations, until the classic vision of extremism and the negative influence that it had in the Army extended to the Republican alignment. In short, the Anarchists, and in general all the Antistalinists, became the focus of defamatory campaigns and ended up becoming scapegoats ready to be physically eliminated. Even the initiative of the Comintern to create the International Brigades was lived by the Anarchists and Trotskyists as another attempt to extend the dominion of the party on the Army, because, among the foreigners who were in Spain, many others were adhered to new units, or were asked to leave the militia or simply gave up going to the Brigades. After all, it is understandable that this would happen, if we consider that regular supplies and more modern weapons only came to the organic units of Stalin's policy. When Largo Caballero's Government fell, and a new cabinet led by Juan Negrín was formed, Moscow's propaganda destroyed any credibility or reputation related with Anarchists and other dissidents under the guidelines of the Communist International, which permitted the political police to use the iron fist and favoured the elimination of rival leaders, generating a controversy that, in fact, has not yet ceased. The conflicts, which exploded almost everywhere, irreparably deteriorated the political cohesion of the Antifascist side. Some warnings about the difficulty of political coexistence between foreign volunteers had already occurred in January 1937, although it was a minor issue compared to what happened next. It happened that a part of the Italians present in the Giustizia e Libertà Centuria separated from the Francisco As-

caso Column of the CNT, because of the dissensions arisen by the election of an officer. In fact, the militiaman Ottorino Orlandini, member of the Partito Popolare (People's Party of Italy), had been proposed as an officer of the Italian Centuria by Carlo Rosselli, but his appointment was opposed by others who did not like Catholic commanders, and someone accused the candidate of Rosselli to be engaged in Italy with the Fascists and doubted his good faith. For this and other reasons, Rosselli resigned from command and some 50 Italian volunteers left the column to form an independent unit, which took the name of Matteotti Centuria, was absorbed by the international contingent of the Durruti Column, which would be in most part transferred to the Garibaldi Battalion of the International Brigades. The diversity of the ideological orientation that characterized the entire Republican implementation generated a myriad of problems, but these had more weight in the rearguard and in the military dome, since on the front there was a cohesive and a spirit of admirable collaboration among the combatants, where political affiliation eventually ended up overshadowing the engagement against the common enemy. Faithful to their convictions, many of those who had arrived in Spain in the early days of the war, fought more for revolutionary ideals than in defence of the Government of Madrid, which, overwhelmed by political rivalry, would accuse them of being enemies of the people and would pursue them as Fascist spies.

▲ Argentinian volunteer Michèle "Mika" Feldman (1902-1992), second right, among other volunteers in Aragón. Since August 1936, she was ahead of a motorized unit of the POUM militia and was one of the many young people who fought with their comrades during the first months of the Civil War. Feldman was probably the only foreigner woman with a commandment position in the Popular Militia, from which he had to resign after the Government bill of October 1936, which forbade women to serve on the frontline. From his war experiences, she left a large account, first published in France, where Mika had established himself in the post-war period working as a translator for the United Nations. (Author's archive)

45 International Division (December 1937)

Commander: Colonel Jorge Hans (Hans Kahle)
 - General Staff Division:
  Transmissions - Supply and Logistic - Cavalry Squadron - Pioneers' Battalion - Anti-tank Battery - Armoured Platoon - Divisional Artillery Command (Grupo Skoda *Baller*)

  Gramsci Battery   *Liebknecht* Battery   *Thaelmann Battery*

XII Brigade Garibaldi:
 Comandante: Arturo Zanoni
  - Estado Mayr:
 logistica – transporte – sanidad – transmisiones;
 Battalion *Garibaldi*: 3 cp. fusileros; 1 comp. ametralladoras
 Battalion *Figlio*: 4 cp. fusileros;
 II Battalion *Italoespañol*: 4 cp. fusileros;
 III Battalion *Italoespañol*: 4 cp. fusileros;

XIII Brigade Dabrowski:
 Comandante: Jan Barwinski
  - Estado Mayr:
 Exploracion - logistica – transporte – sanidad – transmisiones;
 Battalion *Dabrowski*: 5 cp. fusileros; 1 cp. ametralladoras
 Battalion *Palafox*: 4 cp. fusileros;
 Battalion *Mickiewicz*: 4 cp. fusileros;
 Battalion *Rakosi*: 4 cp. fusileros;
 Compañía de ametralladoras;
 Battery anticarro *Petko Miletic*.

Fuente: Michel Alpert: *El Ejército Republicano en la Guerra Civil*; Carlos Engel: *Historia de las Brigadas Mixtas del Ejército Popular de la República*; Salas Larrazabal : *Historia del Ejército Popular de la República*.

▲ Margarita Nelken Mansberger, Spanish intellectual and revolutionary. An outstanding exponent of the feminist movement.

▲ Ernest Hemingway with Soviet and German intellectuals Ilya Ehrenburg and Gustav Regler, possibly working on the propaganda film *The Spanish Earth*, 1937. (JFKLibrary, Public Domain)

▼ A snapshot taken in Madrid in July 1936, which shows the distribution of military equipment to the militia and suggests how quickly the dispersal of the material found in the arsenals extracted to the Rebels was carried out. (Author's archive)

2 - INTERNATIONAL BRIGADES

In early autumn of 1936, it was typical to find a good number of foreigners among the streets of Spain. Most of them were young workers, but also farmers, students and intellectuals, all of them heading to the same destination: Albacete. Most had entered in Spanish territory from the border crossing along the Pyrenees, but others had arrived at the ports of Barcelona and Cartagena after embarking in Marseille. These volunteers had gathered through the initiatives of the committees supporting the Republican cause, whose exponents had denounced the aggression of the Rebel forces in the major cities of Europe. The propaganda concerned, firstly, in neighbouring France, in Belgium and in Great Britain, and was directed mainly to the working classes and the leftist circles, in order to raise awareness among the masses in the name of militant internationalism. The mechanism had already begun at the end of July, when demonstrations in France and Great Britain were carried out in support of the Republic and, therefore, the centres coordinated by the Committee International de L'Aide au Peuple Espagnol emerged. Initially, the committees were sponsored by the Spanish Government through political organizations that supported the Republic, and planned to obtain not only material help, but also to extend the consent of the citizens of the neighbouring countries, so they would pressure their governments to support the Republic's military effort. Soon the conferences organized by the Spaniards joined similar initiatives, almost always under the auspices of the Comintern, to find volunteers and to form an international militia in support of the legitimately elected Government. To expand the initiative, Willy Münzenberg, a German Communist expatriate in the USSR, was asked to plan a propaganda campaign in favour of Republican Spain, which involved the international Antifascist front. Taking advantage of the common ideal of class consciousness, the propaganda work gave good results and the volunteers began to arrive from almost everywhere, starting with France, where many Antifascist expatriates from Italy and other European countries, like Poland -where the left was not allowed any political activity- lived. The activity of the officials controlled by Moscow was carried out in a semi-clandestine way, since on the Soviet Union it was necessary not to expose the State's intentions openly, taking into account that in August 1936 the main orientation of the international policy was to remain neutral and not provide support to any of the sides in the fight. Only after it was established that Hitler and Mussolini were sending men and means to support the Nationalists, the resistance decreased, and the flow of aid to support the Republic from Moscow increased, including the distribution of weapons and the arrival of the first volunteers coordinated by the Comintern, and the analogous trade union organization of the Profintern. The formation of a new Government in Madrid in early September 1936, presided by Largo Caballero, a prominent left-winger, gave a new impetus to the propaganda machine of the International Committee, which extended its activities to organize collections of funds in Canada and the United States. On 27 August, Moscow had accredited its ambassador in Madrid, accompanied by a large crowd of counter-intelligence agents and military advisers, including generals Berzin and Goriev. At the end of October 1936, the first Soviet ship loaded with provisions docked in Barcelona, a breath of fresh air for the Republic. All the materials sent from Moscow were paid by the Spaniards with the gold of the state reserves. But from the military point of view, it was Mexico, together with France, and not the Soviet Union, the first to come to the rescue of Madrid. The French Minister of Aviation, the Socialist Pierre Cot, defeated the obstinacy of the Prime Minister León Blum, who hesitated to allow direct intervention from his country, and in late July 1936, instructed men to send airplanes and pilots to Spain, supported by prominent exponents of the left as the writer André Malraux and deputy Julien Boussutrot, who offered to find volunteer pilots to form the Escadrille d'Espagne. However, the flow of aid from France was interrupted very soon, as, in mid-August, the Paris government joined the non-intervention agreement, closing the borders and preventing the transit of arms destined to the Republic in its territory. Despite this, through the French Government, the Government of Madrid succeeded in keeping open an extremely important aid channel, albeit with great difficulty. From Mexico came mainly light war material, such as the thousands of Mexicanski rifles (Mosin-Nagants made in the United States by Remington for the Czarist Army and then sold to Mexico) with which the Republican Government managed to equip many of their soldiers. The Central American country also presented itself as a useful transit route to circumvent the US embargo, especially by the precious spare parts of heavy armament and aviation. Sporadically, weapons supplies arrived in the Republic through the most tortuous forms, from Poland, from Paraguay, and from Estonia.

RECRUITMENT

Armament, although important, was not satisfactory without an adequate number of instructors and the support of expert troops, something that the Republican Government did not have in the first weeks of the war. With the exception of the Catalan Civil Guard, half of the armed forces and public security were under the control of the Rebels. The Republican strategy was particularly critical given that almost none of the Loyalist officers, and practically any soldier, had combat experience, while the insurgents could deploy veterans of the Tercio (the Foreign Legion) with the rest of the Army of Africa, veterans from the Campaign of Morocco. To worsen the overall situation, there was the fact that most of the heavy weaponry was in possession of the Rebels and, finally, aviation, which passed almost in full sense into Nationalist hands.

The Republic was partly compensated by the Navy, the most of which remained loyal to it. Even more decisive for the Rebels was the absolute majority in its deployment of intermediate officials, which left the Republican side much more devoid of field commanders able to effectively guide its troops in battle. Towards the end of September, the Rebels rapidly advanced towards Madrid and, according to foreign observers, without further substantial intervention from abroad, the end of the Republic would be a matter of weeks. The decisive impulse for the establishment to send units ad hoc in Spain arose from this framework of events, including the International Brigades, which were the most important contribution, since the increasing flow of volunteers, who through a thousand ways had travelled to the Peninsula from the first hours of the Civil War, it could be framed soon in an armed force trained and directed by trained officers. For the Comintern and Moscow, the creation of the Brigades represented in few words the possibility of fighting in an autonomous way in Spain and having a military body able to participate in the war. The Brigades were rightly seen as the symbol of international solidarity for the common cause, the demonstration that workers around the world were willing to die to stop the advancement of Fascism. In any case, the Comintern, according to the guidelines of its maximum responsible, Georgi Dimitrov, tried to hide this recruitment as long as possible, so that the International Brigades seemed to be cause of a spontaneous movement. After all, the influx of volunteers to Spain continued to involve many Communists with an open disagreement with Moscow, especially among the Germans, who had been on the rise in Spain since the early stages of the Civil War. In fact, many of those who had gathered in Barcelona since the summer of 1936 had chosen to join the revolutionary militias of Anarchist and Trotskyist-inspired tendencies, all united by the conviction that the Comintern had betrayed the Revolution and that was now within reach of Spain. Now, supporting the International Brigades project, Stalin could regain sympathy from the Communists around the world and recapture a consensus that seemed tarnished after his conversion to the politics of the Popular Front, and at the same time to appear in front of Liberal governments as an interlocutor capable of preventing an escalation of revolutionary thrusts. Indeed, through the Brigades, Moscow managed to extend its influence on many leftist movements, especially in those where no Communist parties existed or were insignificant, such as the United States.

In an attempt to disguise its real activity, the recruitment centres established by Antifascist organizations were located in unexpected places: bars, restaurants, workshops, private houses, and hotels. But in France, already in the early months of 1937, there were gathering centres for volunteers who worked more or less in under the light of sun. In Paris, the main base was at the headquarters of the French Communist Party, in the Rue de la Favette 128. Other offices connected with this were in the Committee de Paris in the Rue Mathurin-Moraeu and at the union headquarters, while other recruitment sites were active in various parts of the city, such as the Cafè de Madrid and the Cafè Petit Lyon. At the end of January 1937, fifty recruitment centres could be counted in all of France, the most important of which were in Perpignan, Toulouse, and Marseille. Outside France, there was a recruitment centre in Lille in the Maison des Syndacates of Wallonia. If in France and Belgium the authorities looked the other way, the same did not happen in countries where aid to the Spanish Government was hardly tolerated, as in Britain and the United States, or strictly prohibited, as in Central Europe. The Comintern, however, managed to establish a secret network to help volunteers in order to leave the country illegally. The directors of this operation were the Swiss Communist leader Jules Humbert-Droz and the then unknown Josip Broz, future Marshal Tito. Leon Chajin himself did the same in Poland, where he favoured the influx of his compatriots to Paris through Prague. At the French-Spanish border, the Comintern established an office directed by the Italian Giulio Cerreti before the end of 1936, to accelerate the arrival of volunteers. In London, many knew that in the Office of the Communist Party of Great Britain, located on King's Street, one could enlist for Spain. Among other things, it was considered that the transit from England was very important, because no passport was needed to reach France. In other parts of the United Kingdom, the collection centres for material assistance and volunteers had been opened. In Liverpool, Jack Jones, a councilman from the Labour, served as coordinator, eventually becoming volunteer of the International Brigades and political commissar of the British Saklatvala Battalion. In the United States, the local Communist Party directed its volunteers to New York, where they embarked towards France destination Marseilles.

Before arriving in Spain and being considered suitable, the recruits were subjected to checks and interrogations. However, at the beginning there was not much attention paid to the political orthodoxy of the volunteers and, in addition, from the point of view of the Comintern, the recruits could be converted and regulated later. In general, volunteers with military experience or, anyhow, with good physical requirements were wanted. However, it was an important issue not to recruit sympathizers of Trotsky's Fourth International, and to be sure that they did not have links to the police forces, as required by Canadian volunteers, who had to prove that they had not been in the Mounted Police. Recruits did not always meet expectations and, in some cases, elderly, criminal, or other people who were still afflicted by a disability tried to enter the formations. Having to act with a certain discretion, the "word of mouth" among party members was of some importance. To find recruits, many resorted to methods not completely orthodox, as it happened to American volunteer Moses Fishman, who, rejected for lack of physical requirements, was then accepted because of having brought, as requested, ten other recruits. If those who came from "free" countries could enter Spain with relative ease, the volunteers residing in countries such as Italy, Germany and Austria, were forced to undertake risky trips with an often uncertain result, as happened to a group of "subversive" Tuscans in the summer of 1936: 'Last Wednesday [29 August 1936] at 3 p.m. -La Voce degli Italiani (The Italians' Voice), an Antifascist bulletin printed in Paris, said, in early September- a sailboat entered the port of Macinaggio in Corsica. It carried five Italians aboard, one fifty years old, and the other very young, both who claimed to have fled from Italy.' The five fugitives had left Castigliane della Pescaia the night of 27 to 28 August in a boat bought with the money of a subscription between the Antifascists of Grosseto: 'The five Italians - The Voce continued- were arrested and, on the same night of their arrival, transported to Bastia by the local gendarmerie. After a brief interrogation, they were released, but remained available to the police awaiting further instructions. The five fugitives declared to the newspaper's correspondent to be Antifascists and 'without a penny in their pockets'. After rejecting the invitations of the captain of the Gendarmerie to enlist in the French Foreign Legion, the aspiring volunteers managed to reach Ajaccio in some way and from there, thanks to a Corsican Communist, made contact with the Italian Communist Party in Paris. One by one they were sent to the mainland, from where they left for Albacete. Only the eldest, despite repeated protests, was held in France because he was blind to one eye. Another dangerous option to reach the International Brigades was chosen by the recruits Edmondo Della Vedova and Siro Rosi, sent to Spain in February 1937 with the Fascist Corpo Truppe Volontarie, but deserted in the following month of April to move to the International Brigades. The same method was used by a German of the Legion Condor, later enlisted in the Jewish company of the Palafox Battalion. It was the riskiest option, as desertion was punished with the death penalty and also exposed the families of the fugitives to the regime's retaliation. It cannot be determined exactly how many members of the contingent sent by Mussolini defected and then joined the International Brigades, but it is not an isolated phenomenon, at least, judging by the reports of the Fascist police informants. In France, in the refugee camp of the International Brigades, a dozen former CTV soldiers were identified. The French border crossings continued until autumn 1936 by the main access routes to reach Spain and, for some time, the French border guards did not obstruct the transit of the volunteers who, by train or by mail, presented themselves to customs. At first, many volunteers reported that the men of the Gendarmerie responded to the greeting with the raised fist salute. Then, with the adjustment of controls at the border, it was necessary to venture on foot on the mountain trails, or to wait for boarding on a Spanish boat that clandestinely transported volunteers from Marseilles to Barcelona or Cartagena. But even this route was risky, since it openly defied the naval blockade imposed by the submarines of Rome and Berlin, and culminated with the sinking of the steam boat Barcelona in May 1937, triggering the death of more than 500 volunteers. The route through the Pyrenees departed from Perpignan, where the volunteers offered the Casa del Pueblo (House of the People) of the Communist Party of France and the old military hospital as a hotel. Then, gathered in groups of twenty at a time, they waited for the trucks or messengers to be addressed to the control of Figueras, crossing the border with the complicity of the customs officers and the French Gendarmerie. Once in Spanish territory, the volunteers stayed for a day or two at the facilities of the ancient fortress of Figueras, before leaving by train to Albacete.

The commitment payment that each volunteer earned once enlisted was 12 pesetas per day. Without due proportions with the change of then -1 peseta was equivalent, for example, to 2.22 Italian liras- the pay was not negligible. However, it seemed ridiculous if compared with what, for example, the Italian troops of CTV received. In addition to the officers, who benefited from a special assignment at the beginning and then a monthly that increased over time, a simple Italian lieutenant in the fourth month of service received 707 liras, plus 73 liras daily, while each soldier received 20 extra liras for all days of service in Spain. Finally, if we think that in the same period a high school teacher in Italy earned 800 liras a month and a primary teacher, 550 liras, the comparison with the compensation of a volunteer of the International Brigades becomes ruthless. One of the problems attempted to disguise was the duration of the stay, initially established in six months of service, excluding the period of instruction, scheduled for two to four weeks. The war, however, lasted longer than imagined by the leaders of Albacete and later, on September 27, 1937, the Government issued a decree containing the 20 articles of the Statute of the International Brigades, where the duration of the service was not clearly specified. In paragraph 20, a very generic 'until the end of the current campaign' was simply indicated. The ambiguity of the terms of permanence in Spain represented the cause of multiple problems and a source of constant discontent among the volunteers who wished to close their experience in the battlefield. A Swiss volunteer told his commander, 'I came to fight for my own will and in the same way I shall leave when I consider it opportune'.

With the prolongation of the war, it became increasingly difficult to recruit new volunteers abroad to cover the losses suffered in battle, so much that, after July 1937, afterwards the Battle of Brunete, the Brigades were composed in an average of a third to two fifths of Spanish recruits. Of all the reinforcements sent to the Brigades in early August 1937, estimated at approximately 4,800 men, only one third were foreigners. According to a superior officer of the XI Brigade, Ludwig Renn, in January 1937 there were Spanish recruits already in the unit; while, according to Giovanni Calandrone, since April 1937, the Thaelmann Battery and the battalions Garibaldi, Dombrowski and Rakosi had been completed with local recruits, in particular the last two, now only with half of international percentage. In the following August, an article in the New York Times claimed that the International Brigades deployed 15,308 men, of whom 7,171 were Spanish. A year later, in a report written by Luigi Longo, it was stated that the international presence within the brigades was 35% of the total. The influx of recruits on the other side of the border, increasingly small, could only correct, but not reverse, the tendency for the local contingent to grow in the Brigades. Among the reasons for this descent are undoubtedly the unfavourable news from Spain. The Republican defeats were added to the controversy after the riots and repression that occurred in Barcelona and perhaps the stories of some veterans, whose experiences in Spain had not appeared as anything other than a romantic adventure. Although the difficulties existing to overcome the French-Spanish border were partly an impediment for those who wanted to reach Spain, it was the failure of the offensive of Brunete which marked a line of clear demarcation in the history of the International Brigades, and from July 1937 the decline of volunteers became increasingly marked and accompanied by the growth of discontent, especially among those who thought the period of service had ended, and instead saw themselves forced to remain in the ranks. The leaders of the Comintern realized that it was very difficult to maintain the commitment to get enough recruits in Spain to keep the Brigades alive, taking into account that efficient organizations like the Communist Party of Italy in exile sent to the front in February 1938 only 34 volunteers a month instead of the 400 they had guaranteed a year earlier. The shortage of foreign volunteers forced the staff of the International Brigades to revoke the permits and enlist recruits in the rearguard and in the hospitals, leaving the convalescents on the frontlines. The imposing block of propaganda established around the world had exhausted its impulse: the volunteers who returned home spoke about the hell of the battlefields and the severe discipline imposed within the units. After the Second World War, many Western historians gathered these testimonies in an Anticommunist key, magnifying some of the negative events concerning the volunteers to dispel the myth of the International Brigades. But if the establishment of the Brigades was essentially due to the initiative of the Communist parties loyal to the Comintern, this does not mean that the volunteers should be considered as puppets of Moscow. Conservative historiography has insisted a great deal on this representation of reality, a trend that reached its peak in the 1990s. However, it would not be fair to put Stalin's responsibilities and the catastrophic errors committed by the Comintern in Spain, with the idealism and heroic impetus of those who sacrificed comfort, security and, often, life, to defend democracy. The most important legacy left by the Brigades and the international volunteers is that of those who, in the first place, and contrary to the chancelleries of all democratic countries, perceived the danger represented by Nazism and Fascism, and fought.

▲ Insignia belonging to the 2nd "Mexico" Battalion of Antifascist Militias of Malaga within the Thaelmann Centuria, with red and yellow inscriptions with background. The allusion to Mexico is in honour to one of the few countries that from the first moment helped the Republic, although the unit was made up of Spanish volunteers, and not from the Central American country. Still and so, many Mexicans fought as volunteers in the Spanish Army; one of the best known was the commander of the LXIX Mixed Brigade in the Front of Madrid, Eleuterio Ruiz, known as the Meji. (Volunteers' Freedom Exhibition catalogue, International Brigades, Association of Friends of the International Brigades. Albacete, 1999)

ORGANIZATION, LOGISTICS AND TRAINING

The city designated to receive international volunteers was Albacete, a small town in the south of Madrid, where the central Committee of the International Brigades was installed in mid-October, formed by the Italians Mario Nicoletti (Giuseppe Di Vittorio) and Luigi Longo, the German Hans Kahle, the French Rouquès and Rébière, the Polish Wisniewski, and the Yugoslav Kalmanovic, followed a few weeks later by the French André Marty and Vital Gayman. Initially appointed as consultants, they would later act as the military and operational summit of the Brigades. An international delegation was accredited by the central Government, where the initial resistance of the Prime Minister Largo Caballero had seemed to bury the Albacete project, since the idea of hosting an autonomous military force outside the control of the Republican Staff was seen as blatant interference in internal affairs. The Spanish Government's attempts to integrate the International Brigades into the Republican Army were a duel between the Comintern and Largo Caballero's cabinet for a long time. But the aid that the International Brigades offered to the Republic was too important and, therefore, on 22 October, the Albacete base officially began its activity. The Government accepted the international initiative hoping to resolve the matter in due time. During November and December 1936, the flow of combatants remained constant, reaching almost 800 men a week, so that the areas allocated to the brigades were occupied in a relatively short time by hundreds of volunteers. The first problem faced by the leaders of the Albacete base was the preparation of the men and their hospitalization at the military barracks. To accommodate the growing number of recruits arriving at the base, many buildings had to be requisitioned to make offices, warehouses, rooms, and teaching spaces in a hurry. The housing problem was the most urgent to solve, as the three barracks of the city could house a maximum of 400 men, while, in one of them, where there was enough space for a maximum of 200 people, in November reached 1500 volunteers. The emergency forced the leaders of Albacete to request the permission of the Government to decentralise the men to the neighbouring towns Casas Ibáñez, Mahora, Madrigueras, Tarazona de la Mancha,

Fuentealbilla, Almansa, Chinchilla, La Roda, Quintanar de la República (now del Rey) and Villanueva de la Jara. Another important problem was food, as the kitchens that existed on the premises could feed a thousand men at the most, so more and more food stamps were distributed to the recruits in the city. To complicate things, some opposition arose also in the different culinary tastes of the many nationalities present. Later, in June 1937, to resolve this inconvenience, a circular informed all foreign volunteers that, in order to cope with the diverse needs of food, they would refrain from paying 3 pesetas a day. In the first weeks, the logistic service worked among a thousand obstacles and difficulties, forcing the managers of the base to resort to a thousand tricks to cope with the continuous emergencies. In the districts respectively assigned, the volunteers were distributed in platoons, where they stayed and received training. Then, they were sent to companies and finally to battalions. Often, the first officer they saw was not the unit commander, but the political commissar. The strong ideological interpretation that the Comintern had on the Army gave a great importance to the figure of the political commissar, considering it a fundamental element of the military organization. The indoctrination began with the same commissars, subjected to the political commissariat of the Brigades headquarters, directed during the first three years by Luigi Longo. Each unit had its own commissar, so the company's political commissars were subordinated to the battalion's and finally to the brigade's. The main task of the commissars was the indoctrination of the troops, the maintenance of the discipline, and, of course, the correct ideological orientation of the volunteers was given the highest priority. The commissars had to prepare the troops before the fighting by explaining the strategic, military, and political importance of the action to be undertaken, to underline the problems they should face and take responsibility for the task they were required to do. The results of the work of the commissar varied according to his capacity and, if he was a courageous and intelligent man, he could obtain the respect of men and their willingness to listen and follow his instructions. Therefore, we can understand that the election of the political commissars was carried out with great attention, given the importance of their work of psychological preparation of the troops, capable of renovating them into a homogeneous and forged block ready for combat. The image of the pedantic and fanatical political commissar was not always reflected in the history of the International Brigades, and many paid their work with their own life. During the Battle of Brunete, the XIII Brigade lost eight of their ten commissars, killed or wounded

INTERNATIONAL BATTALIONS (Original sheet in italian)

N°		data formazione:	battaglione:	nazionalità:	brigata:	scioglimento:
1	41	22 ottobre 1936	Edgar Andrè	germanici, austriaci	XI	23 settembre 1938
2	56	22 ottobre 1936	Commune de Paris	francesi, belgi	XI – XIV	23 settembre 1938
3	45	22 ottobre 1936	Garibaldi	italiani	XI – XII	23 settembre 1938
4	49	22 ottobre 1936	Dabrowski	polacchi, ungheresi, cecoslovacchi	XI – XII - XIII	23 settembre 1938
5	43	22 ottobre 1936	Thaelmann	germanici, belgi, olandesi, scandinavi britannici	XII – XI	23 settembre 1938
6	46	9 novembre 1936	André Marty	francesi e belgi	XII – CL - XIV	23 settembre 1938
7	47	10 novembre 1936	Louise Michel	francesi	XIII	6 gennaio 1937
8	48	1 dicembre 1936	Tchapaief	jugoslavi, polacchi, rumeni, bulgari, ungheresi	XIII	5 agosto 1937
9	-	15 dicembre 1936	Nueve Naciónes	multinazionale	XIV	4 gennaio 1937
10	50	15 dicembre 1936	Henry Vuillemin	francesi	XIII - XIV	27 maggio 1938
12	-	15 dicembre 1936	La Marseillaise, poi Ralph Fox	francesi, britannici	XIV	26 maggio 1938
13	53	19 dicembre 1936	Henry Barbusse	francesi	XIV	23 settembre 1938
28	-	21 dicembre 1936	Vaillant-Couturier	francesi, belgi, germanici	XIV	23 settembre 1938
16	57	22 dicembre 1936	British	britannici	XV	24 settembre 1938
17	58	10 gennaio 1937	Abraham Lincoln	statunitensi e canadesi	XV	24 settembre 1938
18	59	30 gennaio 1937	Dimitrov	multinazionale	XV - CXXIX	16 ottobre 1938
20	-	15 marzo 1937	Veinte	multinazionale	LXXXVI	10 gennaio 1938
24	-	5 aprile 1937	Español	sudamericani	XV	6 maggio 1938
15	55	5 aprile 1937	Six Fevrier	francesi, belgi	XV - XIV	26 maggio 1938
27	-	10 aprile 1937	Djure-Djakovic	jugoslavi	CL - CXXIX	16 ottobre 1938
-	-	1 maggio 1937	Hans Beimler	germanici, olandesi, svizzeri, belgi	XI	10 maggio 1938
-	-	1 maggio 1937	I Italoespañol, oppure Figlio	italiani e spagnoli	XII	23 settembre 1938
-	-	1 maggio 1937	II Italoespañol	italiani e spagnoli	XII	23 settembre 1938
-	-	14 maggio 1937	George Washington	statunitensi	XV	2 luglio 1937
21	51	27 maggio 1937	Rákosi Mátyás	ungheresi	CL - XIII	23 settembre 1938
19	-	18 giugno 1937	Zwölfte Februar	austriaci	XI	23 settembre 1938
23	52	28 giugno 1937	Palafox	polacchi, jugoslavi	XIII	23 settembre 1938
22	-	29 giugno 1937	Mackenzie-Papineau	canadesi	XV	24 settembre 1938
14	54	30 settembre 1937	Pierre Brachet	belgi	XIV	29 maggio 1938
-	-	15 ottobre 1937	III Italoespañol	italiani e spagnoli	XII	6 maggio 1938
25	-	27 ottobre 1937	Mickiewicz	polacchi	XIII	23 settembre 1938
26	-	8 febbraio 1938	Mazarik	cecoslovacchi	CXXIX	16 ottobre 1938

In neretto il numero conferito al battaglione all'interno delle Brigate Internazionali dal comando di Albacete; in *corsivo* quello attribuito in un secondo momento dallo stato maggiore dell'esercito repubblicano.

in combat. In Fuentes de Ebro, the political commissar of the Mackenzie-Papineau Battalion was shot down by a machine gun while urging his men to attack. In some cases, the figure of the political commissar assumed such importance that they were considered almost more important than the training commanders themselves. Given these premises, it is clear sometimes there were differences between the views of the commissars and those of the other officers, but on the other hand it was considered absolutely necessary their presence, given the influence they could have on the morality of the men, in their combat efficiency and, especially, in the internal discipline of the units, which was difficult to impose on a mass of combatants that came from the ranks of Communism, Socialism and, in some cases, the most radical movements. If obedience and authority imposed on soldiers were symbols of the oppression of Capitalism, the internal discipline of the formations had to be presented in a different way in a proletarian army. Many of the volunteers, especially the young idealists, had run to Spain in the hope of joining a democratic army, based on the concepts of liberty, equality and fraternity, while the political commissariat seemed to want to create a "bourgeois army". But Albacete never hid that the implementation of even very severe disciplinary methods was a difficulty that the Republican Army had to overcome in order to win the war. The differences of opinion on this and other topics sometimes generated many problems, which made the coexistence between volunteers from different political backgrounds difficult. This happened especially in the brigades where political pluralism was more widespread, as in the Garibaldi and Thaelmann. The Republican Randolfo Pacciardi, head of the XII Brigade from March to June 1937, had to overcome many difficulties to deal with his superiors, especially when the latter attempted to establish Ilio Barontini as his delegate, while the commander had opted for Carlo Penchienati. It was especially the officers and the commissars who were not inclined to comply with the superior impositions who led a collision with Albacete. Often pressure was exerted to obtain progress of degree to some recommended individual and this provoked the clash with those who tended to favour more the talent than the party card. At other times, the contrasts between the High Staff, the commissariat, and the officers of the combat units, transcended to cause much more serious episodes, like the mutiny of the XIII Brigade, with officers ahead, who, during the bloody clashes in Brunete in July 1937, refused to return their units to the front line; or when, in Belchite, the commander of the Lincoln Battalion was threatened with the firing squad for refusing to execute a senseless order. The contrasts inevitably increased when men without psychological introspection accessed to the command positions of the units, as in the case of the XIII Brigade, such as in the eve of the Battle Brunete, under the orders of Vincenzo Bianco, perhaps one of the hardest and ruthless among the officers of the International Brigades; he did not hesitate in some circumstances to resort to the execution platoon pour encourager les autres. In May 1937, a company of pioneers was also formed, in practice, a disciplinary unit, composed of alcoholics, cowards, insubordinates, and other subjects considered untrustworthy.

Among the various causes that contributed to the deterioration of the relations between the volunteers and the officers, the distribution of armament supplied to the units must also be considered. The clothing and the team of the combatants imme-

▶ The sectors occupied by the XI and XII International Brigades at the end of the fighting in the outskirts of Madrid extended from the Puerta del Hierro to the Faculty of Philosophy. The defence of Madrid was the first great victory of the Republican Army and also the first success of the International Brigades.

▼ Many flags attributed to the Thaelmann Centuria -later Battalion- are known. The one shown on the cover of the unit magazine also appears in some photos and was probably on a red background with yellow or white letters. The Thaelmann century was one of the first international voluntary units formed by German exiles and Northern Europeans, who, before joining the International Brigades, were part of the militia of the PSUC, with which they fought in the Front of Aragón and then in Madrid. (Author's archive)

diately constituted a serious problem for the men of Albacete. The first material convoys arrived clandestinely from France in early October 1936 and contained a variety of uniforms and equipment of all types and styles. The result was that the units came into operation with a poorly balanced uniformity, and for a long time men were forced to take some militaristic measures. Judging by the existing photographs and the testimonies of the protagonists, at the moment of entering into action, only a few units appeared dressed and equipped in a satisfactory manner, and among them stood out the German Thaelmann Battalion, immortalized to its arrival in Madrid with an appealing Teutonic rigour mixed with revolutionary disagreement. In the beginning, many volunteers had to make up with the simple mono (boilersuit), a working uniform, of different colours, including the dark blue that were distributed to the volunteers of the Dabrowski Battalion, to wear above civilian clothes. Even later, when the same clothes and ammunition equipment were available in all the Popular Army, the drawbacks did not completely disappear. According to an American brigadist, 'the waste of a dozen foreign armies, including the American, mixed with officers of Spanish origin' could be found in Albacete. As of November 1936, footwear needs increased per month to 5,000 pairs in the following spring. Also, the rugged Iberian soil quickly consumed clothing, which put the brigade supply service into a very solid test. It was not until the spring of 1937 that the Albacete Staff independently trusted in local suppliers to order the manufacture of 30,000 full khaki uniforms. Judging by the images, however, both the International Brigades and the entire Republican Army were plagued by the lack of equipment during the war, forcing the combatants to use civilian clothes and other improvised solutions. To get weapons, the Republican Army was forced to work with all available supply channels, including the use of international traffickers. The result was the formation of a little compound arsenal, with obvious negative repercussions on the units. Only by examining individual armaments in the International Brigades we could find both the Japanese rifles Arisaka M1907 of 6.5 mm, as the Canadian muskets Ross 0.303 inch. not forgetting the more popular model of Mauser, the M1893 of 7 mm, made under licence in Spain and the Mosin-Nagant M1891 of 7.62 mm, built in the United States by Remington between 1914 and 1917 for the Russian Army. Equally varied were the machine guns, with the Soviet Maxim M1910 in greater numbers along with the French model Hotchkiss 1914. Another organisational problem faced by the Albacete officers was the classification of volunteers in homogeneous units by nationality and language. The most numerous contingents, such as the French, the Germans, and the Italians, had been distributed in battalions since the beginning. The Belgian Walloons or the French-speaking Swiss were also able to gather with the Frenchmen. Identical groups could be formed with Austrian and Swiss Germans in the Germanic battalions, whose staff also increased as a result of Scandinavian, Flemish Belgian, Dutch, and even British volunteers. The groupings continued to the level of company and, finally, of section, which determined an apparent asymmetry of the units. This ended up deploying very different organic groups. Since September 1936, each Republican Army battalion consisted of three rifle companies plus a reserve company, a machine gun company, a four-piece mortar section and a transmissions section. Each rifle company deployed 120 men divided into three sections of two platoons, in turn divided into three teams; The machine gun company consisted of three platoons of 30 men each with four machine guns. Minor changes occurred in the course of the conflict, such as the insertion of a small-calibre mortar in each section of rifles, but in the end, each full-power Republican battalion should deploy 655 men, including the Staff.

The availability of equipment and the presence of volunteers from different nationalities conditioned the structure of the units at the time of their establishment. As the Garibaldi Battalion entered into action with five rifle companies plus two assault groups -Arditi del Popolo and Il Terribile- displaying 520 men in total, the Thaelmann Battalion, belonging to the same brigade, consisted of only four companies: 1st German company, 2nd Balkan Company, 3rd Polish Company and 4th English-Rusoblanca company, with a total of 540 men. Otherwise, the Edgar André Battalion aligned itself at the departure of Albacete with four companies of riflemen and one of machine guns, plus an artillery section of 650 men. The results of the combat and the organisational difficulties determined in more than one occasion the entry in combat of units with insufficient personnel, so that in the history of the International Brigades many other cases of polyglot battalions and personal ad hoc existed, as happened in the CXXIX Brigade which at one time included volunteers from forty different nationalities; or as in the XIV Brigade, which came into action at the end of 1936 with four battalions formed by only three French-Belgo-British machine gun companies of the Marseillaise, with three riflemen and one machine gun, 416 men, equivalent to the 550 volunteers Frenchmen of the Henry Barbusse. The presence of small additions contributed to form a true linguistic Babel within the battalions, but the urgency of the fight did not allow to regard subtle topics, so the classification in the battalions ended up following criteria sometimes extravagant, as happened when Ethiopian volunteers arrived, and

▲ The engagement of volunteers on behalf of the Comintern reached every corner of the world. The picture shows Tom Spiller, a New Zealand volunteer and NCO in the British Battalion of the XV International Brigade. Spiller had arrived in Spain in time to participate in the battles of Jarama and Brunete; where he was wounded. Once discharged from the hospital, the Comintern sent Spiller home to seek other volunteers, but after the dissolution of the International Brigades in September 1938, his activity ceased. A total of 36 volunteers from New Zealand came to Spain, among combatants, airmen, and doctors. (Courtesy of the Alexander Turnbull Library, Wellington, New Zealand, reference no. 91-261-40-01)

were assigned to the Garibaldi Battalion, that is, together with the compatriots of the men who had invaded their country, or with the Cypriots, framed in the British Battalion, only because Cyprus was an English possession. In the spring of 1937, once the emergence of the first months passed and relying on an influx of volunteers that was considered consolidated, to structure whole nationwide brigades was tried and thus the XI Brigade became, essentially, the German, the XII had an Italian majority, the XIII, was predominantly Polish, the XIV, was French, the XV, was English-American, and, finally, the CL, was Slavic and Hungarian. But the presence of so many nationalities determined that the different ethnic groups remained within these battalions, grouped according to decidedly eccentric criteria. In perfect adherence to the internationalist spirit, the heterogeneous frameworks determined singular cases, as happened in the Garibaldi Battalion, commanded in August 1937 by the Albanian Asim Vokshi. The significant presence of Jewish volunteers led to the establishment of the only "religious unit" of the International Brigades. In addition to the presence of Jewish religious volunteers from Palestine, who arrived in Spain along with their Muslim comrades, in all contingents there were a large number of Jews who had joined the Antifascist front in response to Hitler's and Mussolini's antisemitism. The original initiative to establish a Jewish unit came from a volunteer named Ariel Weisz, who spoke to Luigi Longo and André Marty in October 1936. Weisz, fallen in combat in the Front of Madrid in January 1937, had arrived in Albacete with other volunteers and 14 French Jews, in the words of Longo 'in a sincere and passionate way', and had proposed the creation of Jewish unit as a response to all the insinuations of the Germans that called the Jews cowards. The idea initially had few followers, but later, in December 1937, the commander of the Palafox Battalion of the XIII Brigade, received the order to form a Jewish unit, called Naftali Botwin, in honour to the

Polish Communist condemned to death in Warsaw in 1925. The company included Jews from Poland, Germany, Lithuania, Hungary and Palestine and used Yiddish as the official language. In addition to the strong Jewish presence in American and Polish contingents, estimated at almost 30% of the total, it is reckoned that at least 200 volunteers passed through the Botwin Company from December 1937 to September 1938. The last fallen of the International Brigades was a volunteer of this company, Jaskel Honigstein, mortally wounded in the Ebro.

Despite having been formed under the strategic control of Albacete, once in action, the International Brigades fought alongside Republican units, and, in several occasions, they presented completely Spanish battalions. Therefore, from the operational point of view, the Brigades were inserted in the Republican military machine and subjected to the adaptations and modifications that were required by contingency of the moment. The need to create larger tactical units than the brigade became obvious in the Republican Staff already in 1936. At the end of October, militia units were forced to be converted into regular battalions, forming four of riflemen and one of machine guns, in order to be assembled in formations called mixed brigades, which included exploration units, transmissions, artillery, health, engineering, and logistics, with a total of 3,876 men. The force consisted of a Staff with 13 officers and personnel; four battalions, each one of 633 men divided into five companies, plus a platoon of mortars, a squadron of 141 cavalry units, an artillery group with four batteries with a total of 519 men, a 42-man supply unit, a health service with 145 men and women, a of 345-man unit reinforced with engineers and a transport and logistic company of 138 men. But the urgent needs of the war forced the Republican Staff to redesign the structure of the mixed brigades in June 1937, reduced to only four infantry battalions, with a reserve infantry company, a platoon of cavalry, a three-piece artillery battery, more service and logistic personnel, amounting to a total staff of 4,197 men, including 134 officers and 34 political commissars. Beyond these, there was a platoon of armoured cars for the third brigade of each grouping. Very rarely, however, both the International Brigades and the Spanish brigades could deploy all personnel: at the time of entering the front in December 1936, the XIV Brigade had 2,300 men in total, only 55% of the total expected. The restructuring of the brigades happened in parallel with the reorganization of the Republican Army and the creation of permanent divisions, created to replace the temporary groupings of mixed brigades of the first months of war. Divisions were a response of the Republican staff to the need for units ad hoc able to operate effectively in the various sectors of the front. From the administrative point of view, the divisions comprising international units and, therefore, dependent on the Albacete base were four: the 15th, the 17th, the 35th, and the 45th. In fact, however, the 17th Division was in all aspects Spanish and only because there were foreign officers present in its Staff it continued to be considered international. On the other hand, the 63rd Spanish Division, that included however the International Brigade LXXXVI, was not among those who depended on Albacete.

The victory of the Republicans in Madrid allowed the permanent organization of the international base, with all its logistical and administrative equipment. Two battalions of recruits were also established to form a deposit of volunteers to be sent as replacements of the units in the front. Each nationality was then available to have an office and print, where an informative bulletin was published in the languages spoken in the brigades and where issues of politics and war were discussed. Training centres were also strengthened, which taught the use of weapons, combat tactics, and provided officers with theoretical tools for the guidance of units. Since December 1936, the teaching of military subjects became more systematic with the formation of a real official school, directed by the General Emilio Kléber. All those who were in command positions had received staff classes, cartography and political commissariat. But the urgency determined by the war did not allow to deepen the subjects and the formation of sufficiently prepared commanders languished for a long time. In fact, the lack of preparation at the command level was constant in the activity of the brigades, which caused enough problems and misunderstandings among the volunteers. The policy helped to make the officers corps very homogeneous, as it more often favoured loyalty to the party rather than the objective merits of certain individuals, which resulted in

▼ Volunteers of the XII International Brigade, photographed at the end of October 1936, probably of the André Marty Battalion. The sleeveless trench leather jacket is similar to the British Army's M1916 and was distributed in large quantities to the first units. Under the jacket, the characteristic mono of heavy cotton can be seen, in this case of khaki or dark blue colour. The volunteers carry shoulder straps and ammunition bags made with local natural leather, with belts of leather and fabric, and are armed with the Spanish Mauser M1893 without bayonet. (Croniqua Magazine 1939)

◀ A flag belonging to the Commune de Paris Battalion, in January 1937, framed in the XI International Brigade in the Front of Madrid. The flag was a gift from the Communists of Espinardo to the volunteers of the battalion, who had spent a month of rest in the complex on the outskirts of Madrid the previous month. Its dimensions are 125 x 90 cm, with red silk background with white inscriptions and fringes in golden yellow. At the front there is a French variant of the Republican tricolour flag, while on the other side the blue-white-red tricolour appears. (Museo del Ejército, Madrid)

▶ Luigi Longo, the future secretary of the post-war PCI (Partito Comunista d'Italia, Communist Party of Italy), held the position of chief of the political commissariat of the International Brigades and was one of the main organizers of the base of Albacete, where the complex organizational network of the Brigades was developed. (Author's archive)

the creation of discontent and resentment within the Staff. Having to judge how prepared and trustworthy the officers of the International Brigades were -especially in the higher grades- according of what happened during the campaigns, a picture of few lights and many shadows appears. The main Major Staffs were in the hands of partisan chiefs and not of commanders capable of leading large units: Klebér, Walter, Lukács were mostly skilful guerrilla commanders, more capable for the Russian steppes warfare than for the Spanish reality. Others, like Gal, turned out to be excellent subordinates, proving that they possessed a quality that coincided with the tasks required, but at crucial times manifested themselves as unable to decide for themselves. Others, like Gómez, although young and intelligent, lacked experience or, as Čopic, some showed on more than one occasion to be poorly trained officers. Of all the commanders of the Brigades, only Hans Kahle, who was already an officer in the German Army, and Aldo Morandi, for his innate capacity and for the power they exerted on his men, proved they possessed the intelligence and aptitude to lead large units and manage complex situations. This does not mean that commanders were mostly inadequate or unskilful, as there were multiple testimonies of individual courage and bravery. Rather, he often encountered the need to cover losses by hurriedly promoting the commanders of the companies in front of the battalions, although in most cases, the command of smaller units was above its potential. In addition to Kleber, Gómez, Gal and the aforementioned Kahle and Morandi, none of the military leaders who left the Albacete base occupied positions higher than those of a brigade commander.

Even the collaborative relations between the international commanders and the Spaniards were conditioned by an obvious underlying suspicion and the attitude of the Brigades, as well as that of the Soviet consultants, contributed to exacerbate many minds. Throughout the war, the Comintern became a promoter of the idea of the single Strategic Command, but at the same time never looked with good eyes at any interference from the Government in the management of the affairs of the International Brigades, and never had any interest in assimilation with the other units of the Republican Army, because this would have meant the disappearance of the political and military autonomy enjoyed by the Communist International in Spain. Thus, the International Brigades presented a double face: on the one hand, they appeared as an organism of the Comintern and, therefore, enslaved by the objectives of Moscow; on the other, they represented the expression of a great Popular Front, around which to organize the resistance. This contradictory position is summed up in the attitude of the leaders of Albacete against the decree of the Minister of Defence Indalecio Prieto of September 27, 1937, which integrated the Brigades in the Army, replacing the Tercio (the Spanish Legion), which had revolted. The decree was, in fact, a movement of the minister to eliminate the autonomy of Albacete and, indeed, was a 'punch in the eye', as it was said, but in practice, it was sought to soften the contrasts and to act through the "politics of corridors". The reform had very few applications and was left in dead letter, because it could not in any way undermine the system of relations and power that belonged to the Spanish Communist Party, through the flow of aid from the USSR. The Staff of the Republican Army assumed the theoretical control of the International Brigades, leaving the situation unchanged and, with this, the activity of the base of Albacete continued without being disturbed.

In addition to the ambiguous political role exerted by the International Brigades, the enormous importance that his presence exerted in terms of moral support for the Republican cause remains undeniable. Although, at the forefront, the total amount of brigades never exceeded 18,000 units in the spring of 1937, and therefore, in numerical terms, their contribution was relative, the presence of foreign volunteers was constantly resonating in the war bulletins, and they always responded with an undeniable spirit of sacrifice, entering more than once into the bowels of combat. Since the arrival of the first international units to Madrid, the volunteers were greeted with great warmth and emotion by the population of the besieged capital. The expectation of foreign aid was so strong that the locals greeted them with the cry of '¡Viva Rusia!' ('Long live Russia!') even if they were the Germans of the Edgar André Battalion. Sixty years later, in a television interview, a German volunteer remembered the shame he felt when he saw the ruins caused by the  bombardment of his compatriots from the Condor Legion and how the people encouraged him, thinking he was a Soviet soldier. Certainly, the foreign volunteers were not pristine and fearless knights, theirs is a story of men, and together with acts of courage there was no shortage of negative episodes.

However, its history will lengthen in the epic of the twentieth century, and this explains why, even after many years, the Spanish Republican veterans continued to consider them 'the best men of the world'.

THE INTERNATIONAL BRIGADES IN ACTION

The limited technical and military baggage that the volunteers had was a notable problem in the first months of the war. As some had predicted, that of Spain was a "bad war", fought without neighbourhood and with the crudeness typical of civil wars. Also, for many of the volunteers, there was a certainty that, even in the event of victory, they would most likely never see their countries again, and this concerned thousands of Germans, Poles, Italians, Hungarians, and Romanians who were soon to be joined by Austrians and Czechs. Among the Germans were those who had also had very bloody combat experiences, especially those who had faced the Frei-Korps. Some of the Italians had fought in the formations of the Arditi del Popolo and they knew about defensive tactics and the use of explosives. Its preparation was probably inferior to that of the Hungarians who, in 1919, had fought during the brief "Soviet experience" under Bela Kun. In addition to these minorities, most of the volunteers were aware of tactics learned in street battles, carried out with bare hands or, at most, with stones and sticks and, in any case, almost all volunteers, including the German veterans ¡ or those of Hungary, were not prepared to face in open field a professional combat force led by expert officers and equipped with modern weapons. It must also be taken into account the cultural resistance of many recruits who, convinced of being antimilitarists, showed little enthusiasm in learning the discipline of the Army. But despite their lack of preparation, international volunteers were a first-class human block which could achieve virtuous results when directed by trained officers.

The favourable outcome of the Battle of Madrid has led many authors to believe that the International Brigades demonstrated excellent qualities exclusively in urban clashes and that in the open field they suffered tremendous defeats, forgetting to point that on certain occasions had been tragically assisted by the orders of the Republican Army. Undoubtedly, the fighting in the capital showed the tenacity and stubbornness of the brigades, but in any case, the struggle in the urban centres always favours the defenders. In the course of the attack of the Rebels in Madrid, the Ciudad Universitaria sector was entrusted to the XI and XII Brigades since November 1936. Soon the battle became a no-quarter fight, while the fighters from both sides turned the buildings into fortresses, closing doors and windows with everything they had nearby, including books from the library, placing machine guns to close the access roads, digging trenches, and connecting tunnels. In some cases, the contenders were struggling room by room at a distance of a few meters, as confirmed in the 1960s by the Italian brigadist Vincenzo Tonelli in an interview with a French magazine, who reported to have listened more than once the voices of Moroccan mercenary soldiers entrenched in the same building. In Madrid, the Nationalist offensive shattered the tenacious resistance of the defenders, becoming a terrifying battle that at the end of November devoured whole companies without rest and with an unprecedented ferocity. The best equipment and the preparation of the Rebels were compensated by the numerical superiority of the Republicans and by the fact that the latter enjoyed the defensive advantage. Moreover, the mistake of the Francoist leaders in insisting on frontal collision tactics further benefited the defenders. Years later, Robert Colodny, who had not participated in the defence of Madrid, pointed out in an epic key: 'The nimbleness of the African veterans counteracted with the capacity of those who had learned the tactics of urban warfare during the street clashes of the Place de L'Étoile in Clichy, or with the Germans of the Edgar André and Thaelmann Battalion, which had fought against Noske and Hitler in Hamburg and Berlin, and laid deadly ambushes on the moors of the Nationalist Army under the busts of Aristotle and Spinoza in Ciudad Universitaria'. Much of the literature hostile to the International Brigades tends to highlight the successes in the urban struggles in Madrid, to dispel some myths and to support the thesis of insufficient training, which, beyond

▲ Aragonese front. Attack by republican militiamen, many of whom were anarchists towards Bujaraloz, where Durruti had set up his headquarters on the 26th of July 1936.

the defensive roles, would have mainly allowed the employment of volunteers in ruinous frontal assaults. Certainly, the two brigades sent to Madrid lacked training and, in the same way, the hasty staging of other units caused serious problems, but later, once the emergency decreased, the international battalions received very little care, or controls. In mid-1937, the International Brigades had reached the maximum expansion and the highest level of efficiency, they were increasingly used as elite units and the adversaries also considered them as such. Later, after the high rate of losses suffered, especially in the Battle of Brunete, and with the increase of the disparity of weapons between the contenders, the brigades began to decline. The operations in Aragón between 1937 and 38, especially the conquest of Belchite and Quinto, have led some historians to insist on the ability of the brigades in urban struggles, minimizing other important successes obtained in the open field. The victory of Guadalajara was undoubtedly the best-known field success by the International Brigades, but also other actions of prestige should be considered, like the conquest of Arges in May 1937 by the Dimitrov Battalion, or the victories obtained in Teruel in the first part of the campaign.

Despite the prohibitive climatic conditions in which the offensive was fought in Teruel, the battalions of the XI and XV Brigades rejected the opposite counter-offensive between Muela and Cancún on January 7, 1938, resisting under intense artillery fire and inflicting terrible losses in the attackers, consummated under the crossfire of the machine guns of the British and Mackenzie-Papineau battalions. On 19 January, the Rebels tried again to enter the sector, but were equally rejected with severe losses. The insistence of certain sources about the bad attitude of international training towards the most up-to-date war tactics also derives from some remarks on the preparation of the command panels. Many of those who had participated in the Bolshevik formations during the Russian Revolution came from very different experiences than those who had fought on the Western Front of the First World War. The first contingent was not aware of the combat tactics introduced in the Western Front from 1916 to overcome the impasse of trench warfare and was based on firepower, breaking enemy lines at weaker points or restricted areas, bypassing targets and coordinating attacks from land and air. Indeed, the German officers of the XI Brigade, such as Hans Kahle and Ludwig Renn, had experienced them first-hand in 1918 and knew the tactics manuals published by the German Staff. For the dominant mentality, however, it was that the German Army had lost the war and, therefore, French and British theories were favoured, which tended to exclude the infiltration for the benefit of the continuous pressure in the frontline. This approach, even and so, was not very different from that adopted on the opposite side,

PLATE A

PLATE B

PLATE C

PLATE D

PLATE E

PLATE F

PLATE G

PLATE H

which in Madrid was unnecessarily launched in the assault of the Republican lines with waves of infantry. Although British Army training was oriented since the 1920s to favour the combination of fire and movement tactics by small and agile units, in practice, the teachings taught to the officers were still those established in the First World War and, in addition, there were very few British volunteers who had been officers to in order to influence the orientation of the commands. The strong French presence among the internacionales did not cause significant changes in this approach, although among the ranks of volunteers coming from beyond the Pyrenees were some former soldiers. The Army of the Third French Republic had been conditioned by the trench warfare and was obsessed with fortified lines. All this translated into the scant importance given to the maneuverer combat and the flexibility of the tactical formations. Even the presence of Soviet military advisers did not change these convictions. The approach introduced by the latter was based on the massive attack and use of the modern armoured weapon exclusively as an infantry support. This doctrine, which would have led the same Red Army to the ardent defeats in Finland, was applied almost without exception throughout the Republican Army, including the International Brigades. This belief, however, was not exclusive to Soviet military advisers.

Analysing the tactical problems that arose in the first year of the Civil War, the French attaché to the staff of Albacete, the former general of the Armée Vital Gayman, said that anti-tank armament was the decisive weapon, and that the motorised units were essentially useless, as demonstrated by the Italian defeat in Guadalajara. Gayman was convinced that, because of the difficulty of coordinating the various specialties at a higher level than the battalion, it was necessary to focus on the initiative of the units to positively conclude an action. Therefore, it was necessary to reinforce the infantry armament and to use the brigade units following a logic of staggered units, used in succession to maintain a continuous pressure on the enemy, both during offensives and defences. But these were concepts that after a few years, in the Second World War, would be proven wrong. During the Battle of Belchite, the XV Brigade, even without support, achieved important results with the conquest of well-defended targets, thanks to the simultaneous use of small teams of assailants with the direct fire of its sections of machine guns, anti-tank weapons, and a platoon of armoured vehicles. On the other hand, in Fuentes de Ebro, in September 1937, the well-trained Mackenzie-Papineau Battalion suffered the loss of 260 men between dead and wounded due to an attack made through an open esplanade, more than a kilometre and a half wide. The assailants attacked as they were in an exercise, remained without the support of tanks, and were finally wrapped in a deadly enemy fire. Many of the Republican failures also occurred due to the lack of coordination of the units by the commanders and the inexperience of the latter, who often ordered hopeless assaults, with the inconvenience that this caused. The first major offensive operation involving the International Brigades was the Battle of La Granja in May-June 1937, which took place after the attack on Segovia and culminated in the Battle of Cabeza Grande, at a height of 1,428 metres, which cost more than 1,500 deaths in the Loyalist side and 1,100 in the Nationalist. The internacionales were represented by the XIV Brigade under the orders of Lieutenant Colonel Jules Dumont. Although at the end of May it was clear that the offensive had failed, a last and futile assault on Cabeza Grande was launched. Dumont's men threw themselves into the assault with great energy, but the steep mountainside, artillery, and enemy aviation thwarted all efforts. After the failure of the last attack, the brigade had lost more than a quarter of its strength.

At other times, the battalions were not able to perform their task effectively, because they were partially armed or with reduced equipment, while the commanders in the rearguard pretended the impossible, without realising what was happening in the front line. The annihilation of the Lincoln Battalion in Jarama on February 27, 1937 was the consequence, mainly, of the lack of information about what was happening. In fact, the Staff of the XV Brigade completely did not know what was happening in the front, while insisting that the battalion had to attack at all costs. After the disastrous result of the attack, the Americans demanded the repeal of Čopic from the command of the XV Brigade, considering it the main responsible for the failure. The Croatian commander blamed one of the officers sent by him to the frontline, who would have misinterpreted the orders received and sent the battalions to the assault by mistake.

The different provenance of the officers, combined with the varied experience of the wrestlers, also contributed to hinder the coordination of the troops in action. A volunteer from the Canadian Mackenzie-Papineu Battalion reported that in the International Brigades and throughout the Spanish Army there was not a single training manual and that every practically commander followed his own habits. The Mac-Pap Battalion gathered volunteers from the United States and Canada, but while the Americans used orders and commands of a certain kind, the Canadians used others. During the war there was no uniform method of direction and, after a while, especially when the battalions were on the frontline, the officers were forced to give instructions using multiple languages, so that everyone could understand the guidelines. If we consider that in the course of the Civil War the Red Army's instruction manuals also appeared, one can imagine how difficult it was to coordinate the units. If we add that the Republicans were often forced to use weapons of different calibre, model and ammunition, we can easily understand how many problems the commanders had to face.

Thanks to the testimony of Riccardo Formica, alias Aldo Morandi, compiled by the historian Pietro Ramella, some antecedents in the operations involving international formations were obtained. They are useful to know the level of preparation of the units and what problems arose between the commands. At the end of December 1936, Morandi was in Andújar as chief of Staff of the XIV International Brigade. The unit was in the city, quickly installed and sent to Andalucía to confront the growing threat of the enemy in the south of the country. The 9th Machine Gun Battalion, called Nueve Naciones (Nine Nations), although, in fact, it included twelve, was assigned to the brigade. The shortage of people suitable for public office caused the leaders of Albacete to entrust the command of the formation to a Bulgarian Communist named Stomatov. Obviously, the election had been little considered, though he had fought on the Romanian Front, but as a private. Because of the urgency, volunteers had received only preliminary training, which was the cause of multiple problems. But to find the origin of the episode it is worth noting the improvisation with which the unit was equipped and sent to the front. Arriving by train to Linares, near Jaén, on the afternoon of December 22, 1936, the four-battalion companies were transported by truck to Villa del Río, where the Republican Staff put the commander abreast of the situation on the front. The conversation was very problematic and had to be switched to French, as none of the international officials spoke Spanish. But even in this way the understanding of the information was not effective and caused many of the drawbacks in the following days. Stomatov and his men learned that the enemy was advancing from south to east, aiming to cut the Madrid-Cádiz Road and threaten Jaén and the entire Front of Córdoba. The situation seemed critical, as the Republican forces could not contain the advance and the Rebels were heading to Montoro and the own Villa del Río. The succession of contradictory news increased the confusion: at first, it was reported that Montoro had been abandoned by the militia, later it was said that the area had not ever been occupied and, therefore, it was no man's land.

Then some men informed that Montoro was still in Republican hands and it needed reinforcements. At the end of the afternoon, Stomatov received the order to arrive at the front and to place itself in the southeast of Montoro. The location was indicated on a topographic map hanging on the wall. The command could not supply any other map as the only one in its possession was the one on the wall. It had been created by local guides, who knew the area, and a Spanish officer had escorted them. At the end of a four-hour march in the late afternoon, the battalion camped in the immediate rearguard. Despite continuous transfers, the men received a hot meal at noon, merit of Petrovich, the political commissar of the battalion, who had put the field kitchens into operation. At night, the commissar proposed to Stomatov to carry out a weapons control, section by section, and the first unpleasant surprise took place. Of the thirty-six machine guns, only nine were working. Therefore, the commanders had to trust on the technical skills of the volunteers in order to put the weapons back on the move, but, although they were properly oiled, several machine guns were remnants of World War I, sold 18 years later to the Republican Government, and needed spare parts. The weapons were dismantled to find the defect that caused them to get stuck and an NCO was hastily sent from Villa del Río, which was very helpful. The time was of vital importance because the next day the battalion had to restart the march to reach the assigned positions. At night, twenty-eight machine guns were working, but surprises didn't stop. Once the boxes were opened, it was discovered that the ammunition crates were empty, without any bullets. In addition, there were no mechanical devices to load them. Loading the tapes by hand was useless, because the projectiles could not be fixed perfectly, and the machine guns would have stuck. In addition, men skinned their hands without getting any results. They were replaced with only two devices available, but it took all night. At dawn, the machine guns were running, and all the tapes were loaded, but the soldiers had barely rested. The Spanish officer in charge of attending the battalion indicated the positions to occupy to Stomatov. The orders were to strengthen and maintain the position and to endure the enemy assault. The trucks returned to Villa del Río. On the road there were vehicles with ammunition, field kitchens and an ambulance. As Stomatov and Petrovich began to inspect the trenches, the Spanish officer decided that he would return to the Staff. All of a sudden, gunshots were heard. The Spanish lieutenant was laying on the ground, and soldiers advanced immediately. The men had a moment of doubt, for no one should be there. Commissar Petrovich shouted: 'Republicans?', but they answered with a shot. The Spanish officer, who was not dead, got up and ran to the hill screaming: 'The enemy, the enemy!'. It was a Rebel patrol in reconnaissance. The ambulance, ammunition, and the field kitchen fell into the hands of the enemy. The 9th Battalion was waiting for the enemy in the southeast and, instead, found him behind him, and no one could explain why. The disorientation generated great confusion, but the officers resumed the situation and the machine guns opened fire again. Stomatov sent a company to occupy a farm on the right side of the front and to establish his command post. From that position, he dominated the path from which the enemy was trying to encircle the hills. After a brief consultation among the officers, Stomatov decided to fight in order to remove the enemy from a hill in front of his position. The assault was carried out with energy and, in less than an hour, the enemy withdrew. During the attack, however, the connections with the 3rd Company were lost, but it was judged that, because of the shots, it was still fighting. Airplanes appeared in the sky, which passed several times flying at ground level to strafe and cause much damage. The enemy pushed from the northeast and southeast, but there were no detours and all the companies fought fervently. From Villa del Río, another officer arrived at night with a laconic order: 'Disperse, retreat to Montoro, the enemy is about to complete the siege'. Finally, the connections with the 3rd Company were restored, so a withdrawal plan was decided, but most of the squads had to leave, except for weapons and ammunition. The men were tired, had not eaten the previous eve and had no more food because everything had fallen into enemy hands along with the field kitchen. At five in the afternoon, the retreat began. Two sections of the 1st Company were left behind with two machine guns, but, with the arrival of the afternoon, it was not easy to keep in touch with it. The Sentinels in Petrovich's column saw shadows moving cautiously. The political commissar took a risk and made contact by voice, first in Spanish, then in Italian, then in German, Hungarian, and eventually Serbian. The shadows answered in this language. They were the men of the 3rd Company. Meanwhile, Stomatov tried to discuss the situation with two Spanish officers, but it soon became clear that they had lost all orientation. It was decided to spend the night in that place; it was the Christmas Day of 1936. The next morning, orienting with the sun, the march was resumed, and the battalion arrived at the Guadalquivir. It was necessary to cross the river and, although it would have been safe, there were no viable bridges or fords.

International Brigades; Artillery batterys		
Name	History	Composition
01) Agard	Conferred to the XI International Brigade until December 1936, then to the XIV International Brigade until May 29, 1937. Finally it is classified in the artillery of the 35th Division and it is framed in July 1937 in the II Skoda Group. Dissolved on September 22, 1938.	French
02) Antonio Gramsci, conocido como *Guido Picelli*	With the XIII Brigade Int. From December 6, 1936 to February 10, 1937. Since April it is part of the 45th Division and, finally, merges with the Skoda-Baller Group. Dissolved on September 22, 1938.	Italian
03) Pierre Brachet o Franco-Belga	Enmarcada el 6 de November de 1936 con el Battalion Edgar André de la XI Brigade Internacional, luego, del 6 de December se desarticula en Valencia. Nuevamente con la XI Brigade de June a July de 1937; desde el siguiente August se une al II Grupo Skoda en la 35.ª División. Disuelto el 22 de September de 1938.	Belgium and French
04) Thaelmann:	Initially assigned to the homonymous Battalion from October 25 to November 28, 1936, then, in the XIII International Brigade until February 1937 and finally assigned to the Skoda Baller Group. Dissolved on September 23, 1938. 8.	German and Austrian
05) Karl Liebknecht:	With the XIII International Brigade from December 6, 1936 to February 10, 1937. From April until the following July it was assigned to the Skoda-Baller Group of the 45th Division, then again with the XIII Brigade until October 26 and, finally, in the Skoda-Baller Group. Dissolved on September 23, 1938.	German and Austrian
06) Pasionaria:	With the XI International Brigade from June to August 1937. Assigned to the II Skoda Group of the 35th Division. Dissolved on September 23, 1938.	Various
07) Rosa Luxemburg:	Established in March 1937 and assigned to the 1st Skoda Group of the 11th Division. Dissolved on September 23, 1938.	Various
08) Jozko Majk:	Established in June 1937 and assigned to the Slavic Group of the Army of Extremadura. Dissolved on September 23, 1938.	Slavics
09) Vasilj Kolarov:	The same as the previous	Polish
10) Glowacky Bartosz, o Hungara	With the XIII International Brigade from August to October 1937. Since the following December it is assigned to the Slavic Artillery Group of the Extremadura Army. Dissolved on September 23, 1938.	Húngarian, Polish and Boemia
11) Stepan Radic:	Established in March 1938 and assigned to the Herik Group of the Levante Army. Dissolved on September 23, 1938.	Yugoslavic and Balkanes
12) John Brown:	The same as the previous	United States
13) Italiana:	The same as the previous	Italian
14) Tudor Vladimirescu:	Established in January 1938 and framed the following month in the Slavic Group. Dissolved on September 23, 1938.	Rumanian and Slavic
15) Rigaud:	Formed in May 1938 and framed in the XXI Corps, including the CXXIX Brigade, dissolved the following October.	Various
International Brigades; artillery groups		International Batterys
I Grupo Skoda *Rosa Luxembourg*	11th Division, Central Front, from March 8 to June 24, 1937. 45th Division, Army of Maneuver, until November 25, 1938	07
II Grupo Skoda *Ana Pauker*	35th Division from June 30, 1937 to September 23 of 1938; Fronts Central, of Aragón and Levante.	01-03-06
Grupo Eslavo:	Front of Extremadura from March to September 1938.	08-09-10-14
Grupo Erik:	Front of the Levant from March to September 1938.	11-12-13
Grupo Skoda-Baller:	11th Division from March 8 to June 28, 1937. XII International Brigade until July 27, Central Front. Artillery reserve of the XXI Army Corps of the South, until September 1938. Front of the Levant.	02-04-05
Grupo Etienne:	XXI Army Corps from May to September 1938, Army of the South.	15
International Brigades; antiaircraft artillery.		
Clement Gottwald:	Created in January 1937 in Albacete and sent to the Madrid Front; dissolved on September 25 of 1938	Czechs and Slavs

Using tree trunks, a small raft was built, Stomatov occupied his place with two men, and with them he managed to reach the opposite shore, disappearing from the sight of his men. From that moment on, the situation began to degenerate. A portion of the men went to Montoro, where there was a bridge, but came across with the enemy, who had already occupied the area. Another party continued to move along the banks of the Guadalquivir and, with much luck, managed to reach the opposite shore. Upon arrival in Andújar, the political commissar told Morandi what had happened and also learned of the arrival of Stomatov the day before. Meanwhile, the men of the 9th Battalion continued to arrive in dribs and drabs and, among them, there were also the survivors of the two sections left behind. Attacked by a strong enemy column, the volunteers defended themselves, but finally they were overwhelmed. The company commander was dead and, probably, Commissar Locatelli had been captured. Ensign Zaccaria and a few others managed to escape, reach the river and cross it. Of the more than 600 men

Cavalry of the International Brigades

Creation	Name of units	Brigade	end-reformed
9 November 1936	*Grupo Caballeria Eslavo*	XII	7 January 1937
7 January 1937	*Grupo Internaciónal de Caballeria Garibaldi*	XII	16 January 1937
23 February 1938	*Sección Caballeria Garibaldi*	XII	20 July 1938
4 July 1937	*Esquadron de Caballeria Dabrowski*	XIII	26 October 1937
27 October 1937	*Sección Caballeria Dabrowski*	XIII	23 September 1938
2 December 1936	*Esquadron de Caballeria La Marsilleise*	XIV	16 January 1937
2 February 1937	*Esquadron de Caballeria La Marsillesa*	XIV	29 May 1937
3 January 1937	*Esquadron de Caballeria Lincoln*	XV	9 June 1937
29 June 1937	*Esquadron de Caballeria Norteamericano*	XV	4 August 1937
10 November 1937	*Sección Caballeria Lincoln*	XV	4 July 1938
13 February 1938	*Sección Caballeria Europa Central*	CXXIX	30 April 1938

who left Albacete, only 231 finally gathered in Andújar; all the others had scattered in all directions, had been made prisoners or had fallen into combat. Luigi Longo tried to justify this sacrifice with the following words: 'Although these losses are serious and painful, one cannot say that the martyrdom of the XI International Battalion has been in vain.

Launched through the advancing Fascist columns, it broke the offensive impulse and gave time to the entire XIV International Brigade and other Spanish reinforcements to reach the battlefield and lift an insurmountable barrier to it.

Although many of the incidents related to Morandi were due to a series of coincidences, to say, unfortunate, what happened in the 9th Battalion, however, is an example of the little eloquent preparation of the officers and the reigning atmosphere of Improvisation during the first days on the Republican side, as well as the difficulty of communication due to poor linguistic comprehension. There were countless ammunition errors on other occasions, sometimes occurring in equally dramatic circumstances, such as that experienced in February 1937, when the gunners of the British Battalion of the XV Brigade, in the midst of the Battle of Jarama, found that everything they had been sent was ammunition not suitable for their Maxim machine guns. In other tragic circumstances, the Brigades paid a high price for the lack of preparation of the Republican Army. During the defence of Madrid in the autumn of 1936, it was the members of the first international battalions.

In mid-December 1936, a company of the Thaelmann Battalion was in a garrison of the town of Boadilla del Monte, but it was found amid the withdrawal of the Republicans, remaining isolated under enemy fire. When a section tried to fall back, it was mistaken for an enemy group in advance, ending in the middle of a terrible crossfire and thus losing 23 men. International battalions were considered as assault units, and had to be able to perform the most demanding and therefore more costly tasks in terms of human lives. As a result, the units continued to be used as a battering rams, without exploiting the advantage that could be derived from the firepower of armoured vehicles. At the beginning of the war, the limited time available for training forced the resignation to too sophisticated plans, with the result of sending waves and waves of men against well-entrenched enemies. Even many months after the beginning of the war, international units used to attack according to the traditional pattern that followed a breakthrough, then a halt and knelt, and again an advance. The use of machine guns, in spite of the presence of a whole company for the battalion, did not conferred the necessary firepower to the assaults, given the heaviness and the scarce mobility of the weapons like the Soviet Maxim and the French Hotchkiss and only with the arrival of the more modern light machine guns Degtyarev M1926 or ZB26/30 from Czechoslovakia, it was possible to increase the effectiveness of the assault troops, among which were the International Brigades. Even so, it was not always possible to obtain an appreciable improvement of the necessary firepower. On the eve of the Battle of Brunete, in July 1937, the Washington Battalion sent 604 men with 550 rifles, 27 light and 8 heavy machine guns, far below what a classic assault unit would have deployed in World War II. A high percentage of rifles compared to the number of automatic weapons makes it problematic to obtain an effective saturation fire against enemy positions, a problem faced also due to defective weapons. Finally, if we consider that the whole of the Republican Army suffered of a chronic lack of heavy artillery and planes to attack on the fields for the duration of the war, the causes of the defeats and the large losses suffered become much clearer. These problems were accentuated when the Republican command decided to create permanent divisional structures, which diminished the autonomy of the Brigades. Between July and November 1937, the International Brigades lost the units of cavalry, artillery and engineering, in benefit of the divisions in which they were framed, in some cases preserving only the anti-tank batteries and the company transmissions. However, there were exceptions, since, in November, the XV Brigade still maintained its engineers, while the XIV still had cavalry. In addition, in the same time the brigade was in the 3rd Republican Division and was only transferred to the 45th the following March. If, in theory, the separation of the other infantry formations would improve the flexibility and the tactical effectiveness of the units, this reform caused, instead, a worsening of its military capacities, since it aggravated the inferiority of the armament in comparison to Rebel units. As an example, citing the two main divisions in which the International Brigades were framed at the end of 1937, the 45th Division had three artillery batteries, but equipped with a single 75 mm cannon that went back to the end of the last centuria, while the other pieces were mostly of inadequate calibres to launch cover or bombardment fires. The other division, the 35th, was in better condition, but had to make up with only nine 76 mm pieces captured to the Rebels the last summer. Despite the strengthening of divisions, which sometimes included a reserve battalion, as in the case of the 45th Division, in addition to an anti-tank battery, available men used to be less than necessary. The 45th Division, the strongest among the internacinales, deployed 9,855 men, while the 35th reached 6,800, less than the theoretical strength of two mixed brigades. The problem was not new, as this weakness brings new reasons to explain the difficulties in which the International Brigades were moving. At the time of the withdrawal of Aragón in the spring of 1938, most of the international artillery units, 15 batteries with only 30 pieces of more than 75 mm of calibre, were scattered between five different armies or army corps.

THE CAMPAIGN OF THE INTERNATIONAL BRIGADES

XI INTERNATIONAL BRIGADE

▲José Hugues, a republican volunteer, 73 years old, fighting on the Aragonese front, September of 1936. (NAC Archive)

On October 22, 1936, the 9th Mobile Brigade was created in Albacete, formed after the union of the Jorge Hans (later Edgar André), Garibaldi, and Commune de Paris battalions. While the first body consisted mainly of Germans, including some Austrians, Flemish Belgians, Dutch, Poles, and other Eastern European volunteers, the second was predominantly Italian, which had been completed with a group of volunteers from Toulouse, but of Spanish origin. The last battalion was composed of French and Belgians, with a completely British company of rifles, in addition to a machine gun company formed by the Polish volunteers of the Dabrowski Section, which was already part of the Gastone Sozzi Centuria, that to its turn became the 3rd Company of the Garibaldi Battalion. Three days later, the brigade extended to five battalions with the addition of the Dabrowski and Thaelmann battalions, in instruction. The first unit was constituted bringing together the Poles gathered in Albacete with the compatriots already present in the Commune de Paris Battalion, and it was completed with other volunteers from the Balkan countries. The 2nd Battalion originated from the Thaelmann Centuria, which had fought in Aragón in the militia of the PSUC and also included a section of British machine guns. The Brigade staff was completed with an artillery battery, under the command of the French Captain Agard.

On November 1, the brigade took the final name of XI International Brigade and was placed under the orders of the General Manfred Stern, alias Emilio Kléber. The political commissar was Mario Nicoletti, pseudonym of Giuseppe Di Vittorio, and the chief of Staff was Jean Marie François, known as Geoffrey, who had previously ordered the unit. On the eve of the departure towards the Front of Madrid, the Edgar André Battalion expanded with the creation of a French machine gun section. A company of sappers and a staff were also added to the brigade, in addition to an artillery section formed by French and Belgian volunteers under the command of a lawyer from Brussels, the Socialist volunteer Pierre Brachet. On November 7, 1936, the brigade departed to the central front, but without the Dabrowski Battalion, still without training; the Garibaldi and the Thaelmann, with incomplete armaments, were transferred to other units, and were replaced by a Spanish battalion. The men of Kléber took position in the night of November 8 to 9 in the sector between Ciudad Universitaria and Casa del Campo with the centre towards the Puente de los Franceses (Bridge of the French). The baptism of fire came the next morning and ten days of furious fight began, supported with courage, but paid with a high rate of losses, which forced the command to replace the depleted battalions of the XI with those of the new-arrived XII Brigade to Madrid. On 28 November, after being used in the rearguard to clean debris, the brigade returned to the previous positions. The relative calm allowed a reorganization of the unit, which received again the Thaelmann Battalion, completed with four companies, two of them German, one Polish, and another one from the Balkans, plus a platoon of four tanks under the orders of an Italian officer. The command of the brigade was assumed by the German Hans Kahle, and the Staff, by Ludwig Renn. Under his direction, the XI was sent to the northwest area to defend the Corunna Road, near Ciudad Universitaria, where the perceptive and appreciated Hans Beimler, political commissar of the Thaelmann Battalion, died in unclear circumstances. In mid-December, the brigade was involved in the violent struggle of Boadilla del Monte, which continued for eight days, and the unit lost a quarter of the soldiers. This determined its withdrawal from the front on 23 December 1936. After a short period of rest, the battalions took again position on the frontline to defend the Corunna Road. In January, the fight took place under prohibitive conditions: frost and fog often made the clashes even more bitter and painful, causing great losses on both sides, so that in early February the brigade was sent to the rearguard of Murcia to reorganize. The three battalions of the brigade were integrated with new volunteers arrived in Albacete. Some sixty Frenchmen became part of the Commune de Paris, the Germans and the Austrians were sent to the Edgar André Battalion, while several foreigners passed to the Thaelmann, which at that time had in his ranks volunteers of eleven different nationalities. For the conclusion of the personnel it was necessary to recall also Spanish recruits. Until the withdrawal in September 1938, the brigade fought in all the great actions of the war. In mid-February it was deployed within the 11th Division in the southern sector of the Front of Madrid, fighting in the Battle of Jarama. On March 8, 1937, when the Italians of the Corpo Truppe Volontarie of Mussolini launched its offensive in Guadalajara, the XI Brigade was the first Republican unit with which they came into contact. The battle lasted all day around the union between Torija and Trijueque and, even giving in, the men of the Hans Beimler -name assumed by the whole brigade since February- slowed the advance of the enemy, giving way to the successful organization of the counter-offensive that eventually overwhelmed the attackers. Guided since March 31 by Richard Staimler and transferred to the 35th Division, four international and two Spanish battalions were aligned in the XI Brigade, a total of 3,565 men. The newly-formed Hans Beimler Battalion, created by German, Dutch, and Flemish volunteers from Belgium, joined the battalion of Austrian majority Zwölfte Februar (12. Februar), with four rifle companies. Meanwhile, the Commune de Paris moved to the XIV Brigade. During the Battle of Brunete, the battalions of the XI attacked frontally the enemy trenches in Quijorna, in the crossroad between Brunete and Alarcón, experiencing very high losses, so it was necessary to move it from the vanguard for a new reorganization. Returning to the first line of Aragón, the XI brigade -which, from July, became the Ernst Thaelmann Brigade- devastated the Nationalist lines in Mediana on September 23, during the Battle of Belchite. In that battle fell the tenacious commander of the Thaelmann Battalion, Georg Elsner. During the fighting in Aragón in the autumn of 1937, the brigade was

▲ Penchienati and Giorgi (major and captain of the Garibaldi Battalion, respectively) in the spring of 1937. They are probably wearing the cazadora, a short jacket with a single line of buttons or zipper, of fabric with pockets in the case of Penchienati, and of leather without pockets in the case of Giorgi, in which the badges of rank had been sewed. The heavy cloth trousers were of brown and khaki tones, and were worn loosely, or tied up and tucked into the shoes. The original photograph was published looking at the opposite direction. (Author's archive)

▶ This photo was posted in *The Guardian* in December 2009, in response to a call launched by the Spanish Government to identify the identity of the African American volunteer represented here. The image, once identified, would be given to President Barack Obama, who was expected to visit Madrid in 2010. The photograph probably dates back to December 1936, that is, the arrival of the American contingent in Barcelona, and it is believed that the young volunteer portrayed was among the dead of Jarama in February 1937. After a few weeks of research in the archives of the Abraham Lincoln Brigade, and after an intense exchange of messages on the newspaper's website, two possible identities were presented: Milton Herndon of Chicago and Paul Williams of Ohio; however, some have suggested that it could be a Cuban volunteer who arrived in Barcelona with his countrymen in the same period as the Americans. (The Guardian, 12 December 2009)

under the orders of Heinrich Rau and, with its new commander, participated in the bloody clashes of Teruel. The men of the Thaelmann fought firmly on 29 December defending the Concud sector. Then, from 5 to 8 January, they fought boldly near La Muela de Teruel by the possession of three hills that were conquered and lost several times. Finally, in February, it was involved in the defence of the Alfambra sector. The losses in two months of fighting were very high, but the emergency did not allow the withdrawal of the brigade, which was deployed again at first line on March 9 until the final collapse of the vanguard, forcing it to go back to the south and, finally, to be secured in Favaro. The disastrous Republican withdrawal compromised any resistance, and the remains of the brigade marched to meet the Republican Army in Catalonia. At the end of the disbandment, the personnel were reduced to minimum terms: the brigade could deploy less than 500 soldiers, entire companies had been annihilated. The Thaelmann Battalion counted on only 80 men capable of fighting. The Beimler Battalion was dissolved in order to amalgamate with the rest and reconstitute it with Spanish recruits. The XI Brigade was international only thanks to the veterans who were still in the ranks of those units that retained the original denominations. On 25 July, under the command of Otto Flatter, the war name of the future Foreign Minister of Hungary, Férenc Münnich, the brigade crossed the Ebro and penetrated deeply a few kilometres from Gandesa. For the conquest of this key objective was necessary to attack the enemy positions of the Puig de L'Àliga and thus, after a period spent on the first line along the road from Pinell to Gandesa, the men of Flatter met the XV Brigade and, on 16 August, launched an assault on the target, in a desperate attempt to move forward where so many other Republican units had dragged their blood without any result. Deployed at the end of the month in the defence of the Serra de Pàndols, the remains of the brigade repelled enemy attacks for three days. They were then transferred to the valley of the Venta de Camposines, from where they withdrew to the Serra de Cavalls, unable to defend such a wide position. On 22 September, after the withdrawal of foreign volunteers, the XI Brigade became an entirely Spanish unit. Reconstituted on 26 January 1939 with German and Austrian volunteers still in Catalonia, the new XI Brigade was composed of two small battalions framed together with the XIII Brigade under the orders of the Polish Henryk Torunczyk, who formed the rearguard of the refugee column that arrived in France the next February.

XII INTERNATIONAL BRIGADE

Together with its predecessor, the XII Brigade fought the greatest number of battles with respect to any other international unit. Originally formed in Terrazona and Mayra with the Garibaldi, Thaelmann and André Marty battalions, the unit was under the command of the Hungarian-Soviet Maté Zalka, alias Paul Lukács; the chief of Staff was Karlo Lukanov, called Colonel Bielov, and the political commissar, Luigi Longo, replaced on the eve of the departure to the front by the German Gustav Regler. The battalions expected to fulfil their lines, but the emergency determined by the enemy offensive on Madrid accelerated the situation and, thus, on November 9, the men departed to the front, assigned to the body of the General Reserves Attached to the Central Staff. The brigade deployed 1,600 men, without artillery support, and the André Marty Battalion was only able to deploy a machine gun company and two riflemen. The latter consisted of French and Belgian Walloons, in addition to some Swiss francophones and Spaniards residing in France. A formation of exploratory cavalry, consisting mainly of Poles and Yugoslavs, completed the formation. On November 13, the three battalions attacked the southern sector of the city, in the Cerro de Los Ángeles, a fortified convent that protected the right flank of the enemy line, obtaining an important victory against a fortified position and defended by regulares troops. A week later, Lukács' men replaced the XI Brigade in the defence of

Ciudad Universitaria, where, for seven days, they fought fiercely house by house, defending the district from violent enemy attacks against tireless artillery fires and aerial bombardments. The brigade withdrew from the sector on 27 November to reorganize. Having ceded the Thaelmann Battalion to the XI Brigade, the Staff recovered with the men of the Dabrowski from Albacete and, with these troops, clashed again with the enemies in the Aravaca and Pozuelo sectors. Before the end of the year, it was deployed to defend the Corunna Road, where it inflicted great losses to the enemies during the defence of Boadilla. At the beginning of January 1937, the exploratory cavalry unit was increased by a small formation called International Group of Cavalry. At the beginning of the new year, under the orders of Randolfo Pacciardi, replacing Lukács -absent for a few days- the brigade was deployed in the Front of Guadalajara, where it attacked the villages of Mirabueno and the Almadrones, conquered between 12 and 14 January, although the advance stopped three days later in the Monte de San Cristóbal. On 6 February, the Rebels unleashed an offensive in the Jarama Valley, forc-

◀ The entrance door of the Palace of Ibarra, where the gunners of the Corpo Truppe Volontarie of Mussolini were arrested by the volunteers of the Garibaldi Battalion in the last phase of the Battle of Guadalajara. On March 17, 1937, Italian fighters from opposite sides clashed in a dramatic anticipation of the 1943-45 Italian Civil War. The Battle of Guadalajara was fought in extremely adverse climatic conditions. Rain and frost whipped the battlefield for the duration of the fighting, forcing the units to finance stocks of winter equipment, as seen in the two portrayed fighters. (Author's archive)

ing the Republican command to use all available forces. The brigade, part of the 11th Division of General Enrique Líster, deployed its battalions to defend the bridges of Arganda and Pindoque, where the André Marty Battalion was overwhelmed by a sudden enemy assault, losing many men and war material in the retreat. On March 8, during the fight around Guadalajara, the Dabrowski and Garibaldi Battalios with the André Marty leading, and supported by an armoured company, were sent hurriedly together with Spanish units to defend the Alcarria sector, to oppose the Italians of the Littorio Division. Four days later, they counterattacked. The Garibaldi Battalion, with the other two battalions covering its flanks, received orders to attack the fortifications of the Palace of Ibarrra, where there was an enemy artillery battery. The garibaldinos rejected an attempt by the Italian Army to break the siege. Then, through a gap, they penetrated the complex and overthrew the defenders, who surrendered after a brief resistance.

Among the loot of the garibaldinos was a total of 262 prisoners with a large amount of war material consisting of artillery tractors, three cannons, six trucks, machine guns, motorcycles, food, and other equipment: the hallmark of a success with devastating effects on Mussolini's propaganda. During the Republican counter-offensive, the brigade occupied Brihuega on 13 March and, before the end of the month, supported other struggles in Morata de Tajuña and Cerro Garabitas. He was then transferred to the Huesca sector in the Front of Aragón, where, in June 1937, participated in the Republican offensive and lost its commander, General Lukács, fallen by Rebel artillery fire. Sent to the rearguard of Tortosa, Fuencarral and Valdeavero, the brigade was reorganized with the incorporation of new battalions formed with Italian volunteers and Spanish recruits but gave the Dabrowski and André Marty Battalions to the CL Brigade. One of the new battalions took the name of Figlio, while the other was identified as the II Italo-Spanish Battalion. Under the orders of Randolfo Pacciardi, the brigade, now assigned to the 45th Division, XXI Corps of the Manoeuvre Army, was sent in early July to the Brunete sector and launched to the assault of Villanueva del Pardillo, which was conquered after a fierce fight. Later, on July 11, the fate of the battle changed, and the conquered positions were abandoned one after another. At the end of the month, the troops were sent to the rear to reorganize the units. Pacciardi, wounded in combat, gave the command to the Socialist Carlo Penchienati, who maintained it until the end of the following August, and then gave it to the Communist Nino Raimondi, who commanded the XII Brigade during the offensive of Belchite. During the August 1937 fighting, the XII brigade attacked the enemy trenches in Farlete. Then, at the end of the offensive, it was sent again to reorganize in Binéfar, where it proceeded to a new change of command with the arrival of the Frenchman François Bernard. Transferred to Extremadura, to the Sierra Quemada sector, the garibaldinos fought during the Republican offensive on the front, where it remained until the end of the year. The new commander Arturo Zanoni, second of Bernardo since November 1937, was replaced after the failure of the night attack of February 16, which ended with the ruinous withdrawal of the Republicans, by the Spanish Major Eloy Paradinas Quero. In March 1938, the XII Brigade arrived at the Front of Aragón to counteract the enemy offensive against Mediana, from where it withdrew to defend the Gandesa-Tortosa Road. On the way, an entire company remained isolated and lost, including the Commander Eloy Paradinas and Political Commissar Quinto Raimondo, alias Battistatta, who fell into the hands of the Rebels and were shot in Gandesa on 2 April. By order of the Italian Communist Martino Martini, pseudonym of Alessandro Vaia, the brigade spent a period of rest in Catalonia to reorganize. Three batteries were added to the Skoda-Baller Artillery Group, the unit of cavalry was dissolved, and the battalions were completed by resorting mainly to local recruits. The following July, the Garibaldi was sent back to Aragón to participate in the Battle of the Ebro. Until 14 August, the battalions of the Garibaldi Brigade became part of the reserve. Then, from that date, they moved to the front line to replace the 11th Division units in the Serra de Pàndols sector. They were directed to the assault of enemy positions at the Puig de L'Àliga, known as the Death Hill. The depleted battalions of the XII took possession of the summit late at night. In September, the battle scenario was moved to the Venta de Camposines sector, where the brigade suffered numerous losses in the fight around the 382, 356, 371, and Coll del Cosso Hills. Thus, on September 23, foreign volunteers began to withdraw. In January 1939, during the Rebel advance on Catalonia, the Italian brigades which hoped to be moved across the border reconstituted an embryo of the Garibaldi Brigade, framed in the Szuster Group, with the intention of joining the Republicans forces in the defence of Llagostera, but any possibility of resistance disappeared, and, on February 9, they arrived in France through the coastal road. It is estimated that a minimum of 1,533 Italian volunteers arrived in the French refugee camps.

XIII INTERNATIONAL BRIGADE

Established in December 1936 and entrusted to the German Commander "Gómez" alias Wilhelm Zeisser, with his compatriot Albert Schindler as chief of Staff, and the Polish Suckanek as political commissar, the XIII Brigade was formed by three infantry battalions -the Louise Michel, the Henri Vuillemin, and the Tchapaiev-, in addition to a reserve company formed by Yugoslav and Bulgarian volunteers. The first two battalions were composed of French and Belgians but completed with Spanish recruits. The Tchapaiev Battalion (also known as Capaiev, Chapaev, or Chapayev), which curiously took its name from a character in a 1930s Soviet propaganda film, was led by the Swiss Communist Otto Brunner and deployed with 625 men from various nations. Most came from the Balkans, but there were also about eighty Swiss and a section of Austrian machine gunners, while a company was totally Polish and bore the name of the poet Adam Mickiewicz. According to some authors, Italian volunteers were also included in the XIII Brigade. The unit reached the Front of Aragón on December 27, 1936 in the Teruel sector and participated in the assaults on the Rebel lines on December 31 and January 2. The Mickiewicz Company found itself in the violent confrontation that took place in the cemetery of Teruel, causing its adversaries to fall back, although it lost one third of the total. Much worse was the fate of the Tchapaiev Battalion, which lost almost half of the force deployed, while the Henry Vuillemin was afflicted by the loss and defection of its commander, Major Henri Dupré, who deserted to the enemy lines causing a real scandal in the French Communist Party. The following January, the brigade was sent to the rear to reorganize. The Louise Michel Battalion was dissolved to complete others, although it was also necessary to recruit Spanish privates, like the 250 reinforcements destined to the Tchapaiev Battalion. In February 1937, the brigade was sent to Murcia, to the Málaga sector, where it participated in the unfinished assaults against Motril and Pitres. Then on February 18, it was transferred to the Front of Andalucía and reinforced with a battalion of the CNT. The Vuillemin and Tchapaiev battalions were deployed in Pozoblanco, from where they left for the conquest of Santa María de la Cabeza in early March. The exorbitant temperatures caused many drawbacks to the brigades, but the battalions remained on the front line until March 27. Between April and May, the brigade was reinforced with two other Spanish battalions. Transferred to the Front of Extremadura, on April 4, the two international battalions participated in the offensive of the Peñarroya sector and the conquest of Valsequillo, La Granjuela and Los Blázquez, consolidating the positions around the summit of La Terrible and rejecting the many counterattacks until the 6th April. However, the subsequent conquest of the heights of Sierra Noria failed, and the offensive had to be suspended. The XIII Brigade supported other rearguard battles, fighting against the Corpo Truppe Volontarie in Campillo de Llerena. Then, all the units were sent to the Albacete base. The Italian Krieger, war name of the Communist Vincenzo Bianco, replaced Zeisser as commander, while the Polish Tadeusz Oppman took Schindler's place as chief of Staff, and the Yugoslav politician Blagoye Parovic was appointed political commissar. Assigned to the 15th Division, III Corps of the Army of the Centre, the XIII Brigade was sent to the left flank of the Brunete sector. On July 5, their battalions advanced on Villanueva de la Cañada, where clashes were unleashed for the control of the area throughout the day. The clashes continued at night. The brigade lost the political commissar Perovic, replaced by the Italian Camen, war

▲ The cover of the magazine run by the Canadian Mackenzie-Papineau Battalion, XV International Brigade, which reproduces the insignia of the unit. Each International Brigades battalion printed their own magazine where articles were written and published in the dominant languages of the battalions and, indeed, also in Spanish. The first Italian publication, for example, was Noi Passeremo (We will pass) in February 1937. Another magazine of the XII Brigade, Il Garibaldino, was the oldest among the International Brigades, published from May 1937 until September 1938. (Author's archive)

name of the Communist Giancarlo Pajetta. On July 8, the Tchapaiev Battalion took the trenches of Villafranca to the enemy, defending them the next day before impetuous enemy counterattacks. The physical exhaustion and the losses caused the mutiny of the whole brigade, which, disobeying the order to return to the front, went to Madrid. The rioters were disarmed by the guardias de asalto ("assault guards", the Republican urban police) and by tanks sent by the Government. The revolt leaders were arrested, the commanders were ceased, and the unit dissolved. The XIII Brigade was reconstituted in Albacete on August 4, 1937 with the Dabrowski and Palafox battalions, in addition to the battalion of Hungarian majority Rakosi of the CL Brigade. The command was entrusted to the Polish Communist Jan Barwinski; the ranks of chief of Staff, and the political commissioner in charge relapsed into the same officers until July. As a result of involving many Polish volunteers, the brigade took the name of the 19th Jaroslaw Dombrowski Revolutionary Centuria. The men of the Dabrowski, deployed in the Belchite sector on August 25, were launched to the assault of the town of Villanueva de Gállego with impulse, but, at only 4 km from Zaragoza, they were battered by an enemy counterattack and found themselves under heavy artillery fire in the open field. After three days of furious fighting, the brigade was forced to fall back. Of the Dombrowski Battalion, only 200 men of 700 saved their lives, while the Palafox was practically annihilated. The fate of the Rakosi, which had to regret the loss of 231 men, was not much better. On 11 October the survivors returned to the assault in the direction of Fuentes de Ebro, but due to the conditions of weakness and depletion of the formations, the action was limited to the flank of the XV International Brigade. The XIII Brigade was sent to Binazet to reorganize, receiving a new battalion of Polish majority called Adam Mickiewicz. On February 3, 1938, the XIII Brigade took another position in the Front of Extremadura to participate in the offensive of Sierras Quemadas, planned to relieve pressure on the Front of Teruel. The first days of the battle were relatively violent. As of February 16, the Republicans intensified the attacks against the enemy trenches, and conquered them at a high price. During the clashes, carried out under incessant rain and in a very open terrain, the Republican route overflowed the Palafox and Mickiewicz battalions, which withdrew abruptly. On March 10, all the brigade units were transferred to the Front of Aragón, where they remained involved in the advance of the Republican lines in the Belchite sector. The retreat stopped at Caspe, where the brigade stood to defend the passage to the Sierra del Vizcuerno. As of March 17, the Dabrowski Battalion supported the attacks of the enemy against Caspe with firmness, despite suffering enormous losses. Withdrawing from the front, with no time to regroup, the brigade went to Lleida and was positioned to defend the Monzón Road. The stubborn resistance of the Republican Army did not impede the fall of the city. However, the XIII Brigade withdrew in an orderly manner and crossed the Segre River taking position in Vilanova de la Barca. In the context of the repression ordered by Moscow against the directive of the Polish Communist Party, in mid-April, Colonel Barwinski was relieved by the Soviet Mihail Kharchenko. During the

▲ Volunteers often wore a blue work suit, colloquially called "diving suit" by the militia.

Losses suffered by the International Brigade at the Battle of Brunete (July 7-16, 1937)						
Brigade	before	after	dead	wounded	missing	total
XI	3.555	2.390	165	519	200	1.165
XII	2.134	1.658	78	295	103	476
XIII	1.967	868	278	610	211	1.099
XIV	1.643	1.600	5	30	8	43
XV	2.144	915	293	747	189	1.299
CL	1.910	1.640	121	320	50	491

Source: Niccoló Capponi: Legionari Rossi, le Brigate Internazionali nella guerra civile spagnola (1936-1939) / Manuel Requena Gallego (ed.): La Guerra Civil Española y las Brigades Internacionales.

▶ Garibaldi Battalion volunteers prepare to reach the Front of Guadalajara in March 1937. The Republicans' victory was widely celebrated by the press of the brigades and had a great echo thanks to the propaganda of the Comintern. A myriad of foreign journalists hastened after the battle to witness the garibaldinos victory over the troops sent by Mussolini. A correspondent of the New York Times wrote: 'There has been nothing more striking since the end of the Great War than this Italian defeat in the Front of Guadalajara'. Through these articles the value of the volunteers of the International Brigades was consecrated, but the contribution of the Republican Army took a second place, when, nevertheless, it had played a decisive role. (Author's archive)

Battle of the Ebro, the XIII Brigade was in the vanguard corps which, on July 25, 1938, crossed the river towards Ascó, advancing until the Venta de Camposines. In the following days, the unit was deployed at the Gaeta Vertex, to support enemy pressure on the ground, fighting until 22 September, the day the International Volunteers' retreat was issued. On 1 October a new XIII Brigade was created, formed exclusively by Spanish units, until 23 January 1939. With both the Dombrowski and Rakosi battalions, formed by Hungarian and Polish volunteers in Catalonia, the XIII International Brigade was reconstituted. The commando of the unit was given to the Polish Henryk Torunczyk, replaced on January 26 by the Hungarian Miklos Szalvay, with the war name of Capaiev, former commander of the Edgar André Battalion of the XI Brigade. The new XIII Brigade was deployed in defence of Cassà de la Selva, framed in the Torunczyk Group. Yet, on February 7, after the impossibility to continue the fight, the survivors crossed the border to Perthus and took refuge in France.

XIV INTERNATIONAL BRIGADE

The XIV Brigade was constituted as a brigade before December 1936 and was sent in great haste to the Front of Andalucía under the orders of General Walter (the Pole Karol Swierczewski). Later, in February 1937, the command was changed to the Estonian Joseph Putz, while the Italian Aldo Morandi, also known as Riccardo Formica, was assigned chief of Staff, and the political commissariat was granted to the Frenchman André Heusler. The XIV was initially the most international among the brigades, where, in practice, all the supernumerary rates of internacionales present in Albacete were concentrated before the end of 1936: La Marseillaise Battalion included mainly French, except the 1st Company, composed at the departure of Albacete by 145 British; the Henry Barbusse Battalion was mostly francophone; while, in the Vaillant Coturier, the 1st Company was composed of Germans, and the other three were French and Belgian; finally, the 4th Battalion, Nueve Naciones, included Poles, Yugoslavs, Bulgarians, Romanians, Hungarians, French, Belgians, Italians, Germans, Czechoslovakians, Greeks, and Albanians. This last battalion was a special unit, formed by a single company of riflemen and three of machine gunners. The brigade was heavily engaged in the vanguard of Andalucía, in the Córdoba, Lopera and Andújar sectors, where, between the end of December and the following January, it was severely decimated. The insufficient instruction, inadequate equipment, and the poor choice of officers it suffered caused serious problems: La Marseillaise Battalion lost its commander at the end of the first war action, when Major Gaston Lasalle was sent to the firing squad, accused of cowardice in front of the enemy. The British Company lost 78 men in a single day after being under the enemy's crossfire. Even less fortunate was the Nueve Naciones, which lost two-thirds of its men in less than three days at the end of December 1936, overwhelmed by the Nationalist offensive in Andújar, so it was then dissolved. In January, what was left of the brigade was sent to defend of the Corunna Road on the Front of Madrid, fighting at the Guadarrama Bridge. On January 10, advancing in a thick fog, the Vaillant-Coturier Battalion conquered the enemy trenches in Las Rozas, but it was forced to fall back when it began to lack the support of armoured troops. In February, the La Marseillaise Battalion changed its name to Ralph Fox, in the memory of the English writer fallen in action in Lopera, while the whole unit assumed the name of the XIV International Brigade La Marseillaise. Transferred to the Jarama Valley, until February 16 no battalion in the XIV fought in combat. Then, the brigade went to the assault with his cavalry to the Loeches Road, deployed between the XI and XII Brigades, conquering land where other international brigades had been rejected. At the end of the month, La Marseillaise attacked the Rebel lines at the summit of Pajares and in the Casa del Guarda. In March, the command was passed to the Frenchman Jules Dumont, while Krieger -pseudonym of Vincenzo Bianco- worked as successor of Morandi as chief of Staff, and Marcel Renaud became the political commissar instead of Heusler. In May, the brigade cooperated in the offensive of La Granja, against the bulge of Toledo. The target assigned to the battalions foresaw the assault on the fortified positions of Cerro del Puerco, in the Cabeza

Grande sector, where they launched up to four attacks in two days. At the end of May, Krieger was replaced as chief of Staff by the French Boris Guimpel. The XIV Brigade remained almost inactive during the Battle of Brunete, using the period of relative tranquillity in the El Escorial sector in order to reorganize. The unit, which included the Ralph Fox, Henry Barbusse, and Vaillant Coturier battalions, was then expanded with the Commune de Paris Battalion, transferred from the XI International Brigade, the Henry Vuillemin from the XIII, the Six Fevrier from the XV, the André Marty from the CL, and the Pierre Brachet of recent creation. From this date, the speaking connotation of the unit was definitively determined in favour of the French. With these forces, the brigade took part in the assault on La Cuesta de la Reina on October 16. The Commune de Paris, Henry Barbusse, and Vaillant-Coturier battalions suffered a heavy counterattack of the enemy, resisting at the expense of large losses until the withdrawal, which took place on October 19. The responsibility for the failure of the attack was attributed to the commander of the brigade and this accusation erupted a bitter controversy between the French and Soviet leaders of the Albacete base. Faced with the enormous losses suffered, the men refused to continue the assaults. As a result, drastic disciplinary measures were applied, so more than 200 volunteers defected before the end of the month. During the fall, the remains of the brigade were resented to the rear to regroup. Then, on November 27, a new XIV Brigade was reconstituted with the Six Fevrier, Henry Vuillemin, and Pierre Brachet battalions, always under the orders of Dumont. The existence of this brigade, formally active, but without having dissolved its precedent, has generated some confusion, so in many texts authors speak of a XIV Brigade "bis". In February, however, we can speak again of a single XIV Brigade with the conflation of the battalions, until then divided into two units. The brigade was sent to the Front of Madrid, and was framed in the 3rd Division, Army

8º BATALLÓN TCHAPAIEF XIII INTERNACIÓNAL

▲ The Tchapaief Battalion took its name from a character of a Soviet propaganda film, which became very popular among the Communists of all Europe in the early thirties. Flag on a red background with inscriptions and stripes in yellow. Dimensions, about 120 x 130 cm.

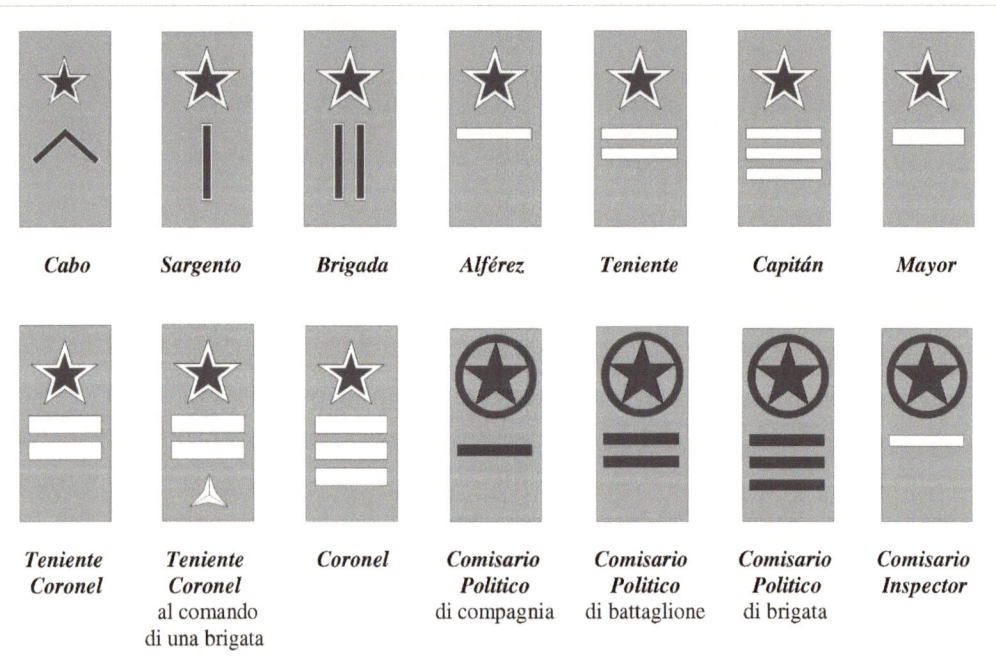

Military insignia of the People's Army introduced in November 1936 (displayed on the sleeves on the wrists, in the cap, or on the chest).

Cabo	Sargento	Brigada	Alférez	Teniente	Capitán	Mayor

Teniente Coronel	Teniente Coronel al comando di una brigata	Coronel	Comisario Politico di compagnia	Comisario Politico di battaglione	Comisario Politico di brigata	Comisario Inspector

Notes: The lower part is made of khaki cloth. The stars from Cape to Brigade were of red thread underlined with yellow; those of lieutenant to colonel were of red thread with golden contour. The chevron of the cape grade was of white cloth surrounded by white; the sergeant and Brigade rods, of red thread with yellow contour; the upper grades, all golden thread. The stars and the bars of the rank of the political commissaries were of red thread, whereas the bars of the inspector commissioners were of golden thread. The command of a Brigade, entrusted in certain cases to a major, was indicated by a three-pointed star of silver wire, two stars identified a division commander, and three an Army Corps commander.

Corps of the Centre. Sent hastily to the Caspe sector under the orders of the French Colonel Marcel Sagnier, since March 1938, La Marseillaise had to carry the Republican attempts to dampen the enemy advance in the Front of Aragón, defending the violent assaults enemies in the lines over the Guadalupe River, then retiring to Matarraña. Losses in combat and defections reduced entire units to a few dozen combatants. During the fights in the Guadalupe River, the Vaillant Coturier Battalion lost 370 men in a couple of days of a total of 450 troops. The Commune de Paris Battalion went from 440 men to only 83 between April and May. In an effort to establish a defensive line, what remained of the XIV Brigade mixed with the remains of the XI, was intrenched in Xerta, and covered the withdrawal of the Republican Army of the Ebro until April 18. Reduced to less than a quarter of the total force, with wholly annihilated companies, the brigade was reorganized in May and June in four battalions, fusing Pierre Brachet, Ralph Fox, Six Fevrier, and Henry Vuillemin. To complete the brigade, it resorted to a massive impressment of Spanish recruits. They were sent to the frontline in the Ebro offensive, where the brigade had to pay again a high price.

On July 25, during an assault on enemy positions in Amposta, the Henry Barbusse, Commune de Paris, and André Marty battalions lost in one day almost 600 men. The Vaillant-Coturier crossed the river in the same sector, but some boats tipped over and only 45 men managed to reach the opposite shore. Some volunteers drowned, and others disappeared. Even so, the XIV Brigade redeemed its reputation as an undisciplined unit by fighting with cholera within the bridgehead, inflicting great losses on its adversaries. At the time of the retreat of the Front of the Ebro at the end of September, of the thousands of men who had crossed the river, most had fallen in combat or were in hospital, and only a hundred could continue the fight. For the value shown in the Ebro, the battalion Commune de Paris received a gold medal. The brigade supported the last clash in September 1938 at the Gaeta Vertex. In October 1938, a group of French and Belgians of La Marseillaise joined the Italians of the reconstituted XII International Brigade to attempt an extreme last stand in Catalonia.

XV INTERNATIONAL BRIGADE

On January 31, 1937, the XV International Brigade was created in Mahora, composed of the battalions of English speaking majority Sak-

▲ Randolfo Pacciardi (1899-1991), commander of the Garibaldi Battalion and later the XII Brigade, with a waterproof jacket padded with leather, similar to another distributed to the officers of the first brigades units, and a khaki pasamontañas with the insignia of major general of the Spanish Army, but of the type used until September 1936. Unlike other Italian Antifascists in exile, Pacciardi initially did not participate in the formation of volunteer units, because he opposed working for a foreign side and only in October 1936 he joined the constitutive agreement of the Italian Antifascist Legion, born in Paris under the political patronage of the Socialist, Communist and Republican parties. Appointed as Commander of the Legion dedicated to Giuseppe Garibaldi, Pacciardi arrived in Albacete at the end of the month, remaining in front of the battalion and then the Brigade until June 1937. (Courtesy of Instituto Storico Grossetano della Resistenza e dell'Età Contemporanea)

▶ In the foreground, three volunteers of the battalion of German majority Edgar André, XI International Brigade, photographed in the rear of the Front of Guadalajara, in the spring of 1937. The dark blue monos, in the centre, used on trousers with belt from the Regular Army, were alternated with shirts of various khakis or beiges, according to the different uniforms' characteristics of the international units. (Deutsches Bundesarchiv, Zentralbild, 183-H28682)

◀ Volunteers of the Dabrowski Battalion, XIII International Brigade, with company leaders; Winter of 1937-38. Since the spring of 1937, every battalion of the Republican Army had a red-yellow-violet flag corresponding to the national flag. In the International Brigades these signs replaced, most of the time, the original flags of the first voluntary formations. Within each battalion, the companies carried a guide, of which different types are known, used for identification purposes in field operations. Some international units received new badges as a gift from the people of Madrid. *(Author's archive)*

▼ A group of French volunteers from the XIV Brigade, 14 February 1937. Most soldiers are shown wearing Adrian helmets and heavy jackets similar to a tabardo. In the centre, most likely an officer can be observed, with a beret with a three-pointed red star, a symbol adopted by the International Brigades. *(Author's archive)*

latvala and Lincoln, the French-Hispanic-Slavic Six Fevrier, Español (Spanish), and Dimitrov battalions, and the Spanish Galindo Battalion. The command of the unit was entrusted to the Hungarian Janosz Galicz, known as "Gal". The Briton George Nathan was the first chief of Staff and the Yugoslav Vladimir Čopic, political commissar. The completion of the combat force was particularly laborious and not all the battalions arrived at the precise personnel, due also to minor drawbacks with the incompatibility of the present nationalities. Among them, note the case of the Irish Connolly Company, whose members did not like to fight in a unit commanded by British officers, and therefore they were assigned the Lincoln Battalion. The Croatian Čopic replaced Gal on the eve of the Battle of Jarama and wagered the French Barthel instead. Deployed on the left flank of the Republican defensive line, the brigade supported the first clash on February 11, 1937, in the bend of the road to Morata in San Martín de la Vega, in the Jarama Valley. The British Saklatvala Battalion, which deployed three riflemen companies and a machine gun with a total of 470 men, was sent to defend a hill that would later be known as "suicide hill", and, after two days of intense fighting, concluded with only 160 men capable of fighting.

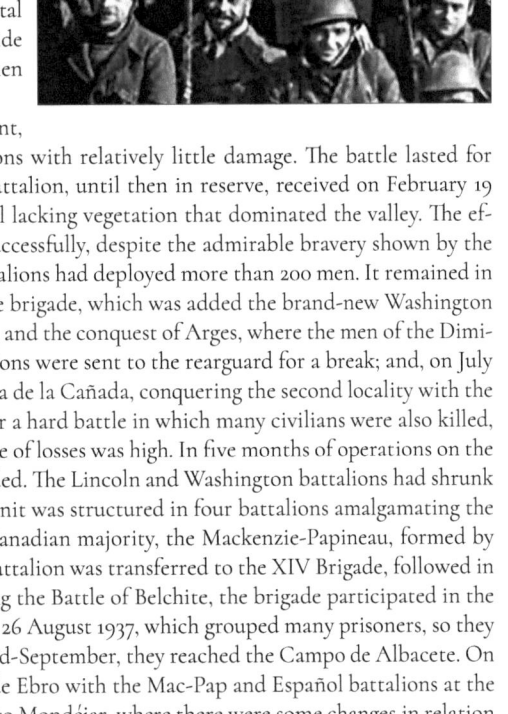

The losses suffered in the Six Fevrier were minor, but still significant, while the Dimitrov and Español battalions maintained their positions with relatively little damage. The battle lasted for three weeks and involved all the units of the brigade: the Lincoln Battalion, until then in reserve, received on February 19 the order to storm the enemy trenches in the Pingarrón, a barren hill lacking vegetation that dominated the valley. The efforts were repeated on 23 and 27 February against this objective, unsuccessfully, despite the admirable bravery shown by the young American volunteers. At the end of the battle, none of the battalions had deployed more than 200 men. It remained in defence of the positions in the Jarama Valley until the end of May. The brigade, which was added the brand-new Washington Battalion, participated in the fighting in Morata de Tajuña, Garabitas, and the conquest of Arges, where the men of the Dimitrov were distinguished during the decisive assault. In June, all battalions were sent to the rearguard for a break; and, on July 5, the brigade departed to attack the villages of Brunete and Villanueva de la Cañada, conquering the second locality with the men of the XIII Brigade. The next day, Brunete also fell, assaulted after a hard battle in which many civilians were also killed, used as human shields by the Rebels in their retreat. Again, the balance of losses was high. In five months of operations on the front, the brigade had lost 1,259 men between the dead and the wounded. The Lincoln and Washington battalions had shrunk to less than half of the original force. Sent to Tajuna to regroup, the unit was structured in four battalions amalgamating the Lincoln and Washington, receiving in mid-July a new battalion of Canadian majority, the Mackenzie-Papineau, formed by four companies of riflemen plus a company of guns. The Six Fevrier Battalion was transferred to the XIV Brigade, followed in September by the Dimitrov, which became part of the CXXIX. During the Battle of Belchite, the brigade participated in the conquest of Quinto, at the assault of Cerro Pulburell, between 24 and 26 August 1937, which grouped many prisoners, so they were left to the defence of the Aragonese city. That, from where, in mid-September, they reached the Campo de Albacete. On October 11, the 15th Brigade was launched for the assault of Fuentes de Ebro with the Mac-Pap and Español battalions at the head. Later, at the end of the month, it was withdrawn and sent back to Mondéjar, where there were some changes in relation to the staff and political commissariat, entrusted to the American Robert Merriman and his compatriot Steve Nelson. During the Nationalist offensive in Teruel, the brigade was framed in the 35th Division, V Corps of the Army of Maneuver, participating in the defence of the Alfambra sector in December. Then, in mid-January 1938, it was deployed in La Muela, where it resisted until the fall of Teruel. In the following March, the battalions of the XV were located in the sector of Belchite, just at the point where the Rebel offensive in Aragón was concentrated. Under intense bombardment, and exposed to continuous attacks, the men of the XV Brigade returned to Caspe, forming the Republican rearguard, risking itself more than once to be surrounded. On March 30, the retreat stopped and the XV Brigade, exhausted, was sent to defend the city of Calaceite. Even there the fight was very tough, where the four battalions were reduced to a force of only 600 men. The British Battalion lost a whole company and surrendered after being surrounded by the tanks of the Italian Corpo Truppe Volontarie. On April 2, the order came to retreat to Gandesa and finally crossing to the left bank of the Ebro. The brigade, was reconstituted with the reintegration of convalescent volunteers, mixing the Español Battalion with the Lincoln, and completed with Catalan recruits, crossed on July 25th the river near Ascó and participated in the conquest of important objectives.

It then directed his advance towards Corbera, participating in the bloody assaults against the Puig de L'Àliga, the infamous "pico de la muerte" ("death hill"). On July 27, the British Battalion, supported by the Mackenzie-Papineau, managed to conquer the enemy's advanced positions. The next day, the Lincoln jumped into the attack, getting some progress. Then on July 29, the British and Mac-Pap battalions attacked again the enemy lines on its flank, passing a steep ravine called the Barranco d'en Pon. At the end of the fierce struggle, on August 1, the "pico de la muerte" was finally conquered. Five days later, the brigade withdrew from the front, but two weeks later it was summoned and deployed with urgency in defence of the area of Pàndols, where the Lincoln Battalion repelled the violent assaults of the Hill 666. On September 6, the decimated battalions of the brigade were in the Venta de Camposines, where the enemy offensive was concentrated and where four times the trenches of the Hill 343 changed of possession. The last confrontation took place south of Gandesa, when, from 21 to 23 September, the brigade was bombarded by enemy artillery and aviation. On 22 September, the order to withdraw international volunteers arrived at the XV Brigade, which, however, remained one more day to defend the trenches of Hill 281.

▲ A group of volunteers from the XI Brigade, veterans, and wounded of the defence of Madrid, photographed in the Plaça Catalunya of Barcelona in the beginning of 1937. The health service of the International Brigades was born in October 1936, initially composed of only six doctors, who joined students, voluntary nurses and finally, authentic luminaries of world fame. Under the direction of the Brigade's command, hospitals appeared in December 1936 in Albacete and Murcia, and a transfusion service was run in Madrid, led by Canadian specialist Norman Bethune. The most important help was collected in the U.S. From October 1936, with the contribution of a group of Hollywood actors and some college garrisons under the chairmanship of Walter Cannon of Harvard Medical School, the US medical office was founded to help the Spanish democracy and, since January, 117 nurses and physicians arrived in Spain. With this contribution, equipped health centres were installed in the rearguard, which saved the lives of hundreds of soldiers. In convalescence, the international volunteers were sent to the coastal resorts of Cartagena and Barcelona, while some of the most serious wounded were treated to the Soviet Union. The Bulgarian Oskar Telge, pseudonym of Tsevetan Křišťanov, head of the health service of the International Brigades, at the end of 1937, quantified staff and equipment of the centre as 212 physicians, 550 nurses, 600 carriers, 5,600 beds, 13 surgical equipment, 120 ambulances and 30 to 40 trucks, and 128 motorcycles and bicycles. *(Archives of Contemporary History - ETH Zurich)*

LXXXVI INTERNATIONAL BRIGADE

The need for new troops in the front of the Battle of Guadalajara gave rise to the formation of this brigade, which, despite being considered international, was indeed a mixed brigade of the Republican Army, annexed to the 20th (Veinte) International Battalion. This unit was formed in Albacete in the spring of 1937 with two companies of riflemen and one of machine guns, consisting of British, American, French, Bulgarian, and Yugoslav volunteers. The command was entrusted to Aldo Morandi, and the political commissariat to the young American Communist John Gates. In March 1937, it was framed together

◄ Thaelmann Battalion volunteers portrayed during a break during the struggles around Madrid in November 1936. Some soldiers wear the M1926 Spanish helmet painted in light grey, without any insignia and with brown leather straps, khaki jackets, and brown leather holders. The individual armament consists of Lee-Enfield M1895-1913 rifles of 7.7 mm (0.303), quite common in the Front of Madrid. The Thaelmann was the first officially constituted battalion of the International Brigades and had already received sufficiently homogeneous equipment in the previous months, while it was framed in the Carlos Marx Column of the PSUC. The men of the Thaelmann Battalion earned the reputation of determined combatants, widely confirmed in the bitter struggle to defend the Republican capital. (Author's archive)

with two Spanish brigades in the 63rd Division of the VIII Army Corps in the Front of Extremadura, remaining there until December. In January 1938 the international battalion was divided to form three new units, but the shortage of recruits made the project impossible and all foreigners were reassigned to the XIII, XIV, and XV international brigades.

CL INTERNATIONAL BRIGADE

Formed in Albacete on May 27, 1937 with the Rákosi Mátyás Battalion of Hungarian majority, the Yugoslavian Djure Djakovich, the Dabrowski and, at the end of June, the André Marty, this brigade was ephemeral, since a few months later it was dissolved, and the battalions were distributed between the XIII, the XV, the CXXIX, and the XIV Brigades in a process of reorganization. While they were framed in the CL Brigade, the four battalions participated in the Battle of Brunete, remaining in the sector until the dissolution of the unit in early August 1937.

CXXIX INTERNATIONAL BRIGADE

On February 13, 1938, the last international brigade, called 40 Naciones, due to the wide variety of nationalities of the volunteers, was established in Chillón, although it was mainly composed of Poles, Czechs, and Yugoslavs. The command was given to the Polish Wacek Komar, former veteran of the Dabrowski Battalion; as a political commissar and chief of

▼ Many flags belonging to the Dabrowsky Battalion are known. This was donated by the Polish Communist Party in May 1937, and in the upper right corner it contains the Republican tricolour, with the translation into Spanish of the Polish revolutionary slogan of 1831 'Za naszą i waszą wolność'. The background of the flag is red with white inscriptions; dimensions, 188 x 130 cm. (Exhibition Volunteers of Freedom, International Brigades, Association of Friends of the International Brigades. Albacete, 1999)

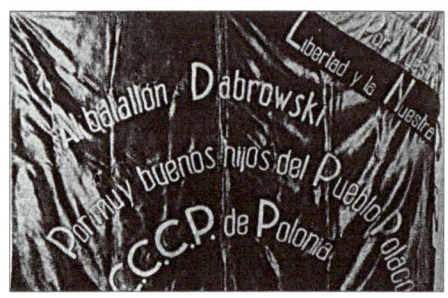

Staff, the Spaniards Lorenzo González del Campo and Major of Militas Massanés. The unit came into operation with the deployment of the Dimitrov Battalion of the XV Brigade, in addition to the Djakovich Djure with the newly formed Mazarik Battalion, sent to the Front of Andalusia, to the Castuera sector, to be sent hastily to the Front of Levante, in Aragón, against the Rebel offensive in early March. With the superior orders of the Major of Militias Mora, the brigade was entrenched between the Ventorrillo and Morella, where it boldly rejected the enemy attacks from March 25 to April 4. Then it was sent to the rearguard of the Republican Army and, despite suffering many losses, managed to return in good condition to San Mateo. Reorganized and completed with Spanish recruits, the CXXIX formed the 39th Dvision of the XVI Army Corps together with two other Republican brigades, fighting from June to July 1938 in the Sierra de Javalambre. At the end of the fight of Alto del Buitre and Fuerte de San Cristóbal, the three battalions were decorated with a medal for bravery. Unable to meet with other international units deployed in Catalonia, the brigade remained in the southern sector of the front and many foreign fighters withdrew from the frontline starting the 16th October. A part of the demobilized volunteers concentrated in Valencia, from where they arrived in Catalonia by sea and, in January 1939, tried to reform an international brigade under the orders of the Czech Commander Pavel. After a period committed to the defence of Vic, the volunteers arrived at Llagostera to cover the Republican retreat and from there they passed the French border in mid-February 1939.

◀ Volunteers of the Dimitrov Battalion, framed in the XV Brigade and, later, in the CXXIX, photographed in September 1937. They can be seen wearing a wide range of uniforms ranging from jumpsuits to a long double-breasted leather jacket. All volunteers wear Adrian helmets, and light grey and brown leather straps of local manufacture. The battalion consisted mainly of Bulgarian, Romanian, Polish, and Czechoslovakian volunteers, including an Italian company. (Author's archive)

▼ Some volunteers of the XI International Brigade, probably of the Edgar André Battalion, photographed during the combats in Ciudad Universitaria, Madrid, in December 1936. It shows the great variety of equipment delivered to the brigade, constituted abruptly in early October. About uniforms, a volunteer reported that at the base of the Brigades in Albacete clothes of a dozen foreign armies, mixed with others of Spanish or civil origin could be found. (Author's archive)

BALANCE

The problem of numbering the men and women within International Brigades will probably never be resolved. In any case, we must exclude manifestly exaggerated figures made by Franco's propaganda that circulated after the war, which cited '120,000 subversives foreigners'. The most reasonable approach would be reckoning around 36,000 men in the Brigades, excluding men who served out of the trenches in several units, such as drivers and doctors, or women who registered as nurses. During to the Battle of Madrid, the first two International Brigades totaled around 3,500 people in total, and probably between 6,000 and 8,000 volunteers had arrived in Spain at the end of November 1936. One of the commanders of the brigade, the French Vital Gayman, estimated that at least 24,000 men had passed through the Albacete base at the end of July 1937.

According to another international commander, the German Zeissler, alias General Gómez, between November and April 1938, almost 52,000 volunteers passed through Albacete, including 18,714 from November 1936 to March 1937; other 6,017 from April to July 1937; 7.781 from August to October 1937; and 19,472 from November 1937 to April 1938. These figures, however, do not clarify whether they are foreign recruits or whether even the calculation included injured volunteers, registered at least twice at the base. Only after the opening of the Muscovite archives of the Comintern was it possible to create a more accurate image of the foreign participation and to obtain an objective confirmation of the number of personnel in the 24 months of activity of the International Brigades. According to data collected in Moscow, the total number of volunteers would have been of 31,237. This numbers would include all the volunteers who moved from abroad to Albacete, and, later, to Barcelona from August 1936 until September 1938. Unfortunately, this figure does not clarify the circumstances of those who joined the Brigades but were already in Spain before its creation. In addition, these statistics would not include approximately 4,000 officers, commissars and other service personnel from the Brigades' base. Even after the new findings came to light, doubts persisted regarding the actual origin of the volunteers. In the mid-nineties, American historian Michael W. Jackson analyzed in his essay Fallen Sparrows: The International Brigades in the Spanish Civil War all the numbers related to the Brigades, its origin, the rate of losses, its age spectrum and ideology, concluding that any estimation of the number of nationalities involved should be taken with a gJanuaryus approximation. As Jackson himself pointed out, to make it more difficult, there is both the presence of foreign volunteers framed in the militia, as well as many Hispanic Americans and natives, that were framed in the Republican Army and then confused with other Spanish recruits. Other problems appear from the comparison of data recorded in the concentration camps after September

1938, where the number of certain nationalities decreases considerably, especially with German, Italian, and Eastern Europe volunteers. This could be the effect of an incomprehensible reluctance to be identified, for fear of being extradited to the countries of origin, or, in any case, an attempt to make identification problematic to the political police. The scarcity of sources makes it difficult to establish the nationality of many volunteers, especially those from countries that are a destination for multinational immigration, such as France, Canada, and the United States. Most of the volunteers left little evidence of their activity during the war, except the wounded and killed in combat. However, the American contingent is, in many ways, a characteristic sample, both because it was the group that included a large number of university students and professors, of whom we know many details, as because through the peculiar ethnic composition we understand well which the various nationalities within the Brigades were. Thanks to the work of the Abraham Lincoln Brigade Archives (ALBA), it is possible to rebuild the origin and, at times, the birthplace of the 2,632 registered volunteers.

Based on a sample of 400 names, equivalent to approximately 15% of the total, it follows that 249 volunteers were Anglo-Saxon or African-American and probably American for more than one generation. With respect to the remaining 151 volunteers, it is instead referred to emigrants or children of emigrants. Among the latter, the presence of Italian Americans (39) and Hispanics (29) is very high, followed by 12 Greeks, 9 Germans, 5 Finns, 4 Poles, two Hungarians, as well as Latvians, Estonians, Chinese, and Ukrainians. 18 other names belong to individual nationalities, including a Japanese, while the other 34 are not determinant, but are likely to be newly immigrated Americans. At least 43 volunteers, 15 of whom were born in the United States, are clearly of Jewish origin. Once they arrived in Spain, the non-Anglo-Saxon volunteers probably chose to meet with their countrymen, so some of the Italian Americans ended up in the Garibaldi Brigade, while the Poles met their compatriots in the Dabrowski. Conversely, Finnish arrivals from the United States went on to form the Finnish section in the Machine Gun Company of the Canadian Mackenzie-Papineau Battalion, further complicating the calculation of nationalities. Another variant that leads to overwhelming the issue is represented by those volunteers, especially American Jews, who had changed their name, as did the volunteer John Murra, also known as Isaac Lipschitz, born in 1916 in Ukraine, who became a U.S. citizen in 1933.

Equally vague are the estimations of the losses suffered by the International Brigades, calculated in 9,934 dead and 7,686 wounded, especially with respect to the significant differences between the different nationalities. In front of more than 2,000 fallen Germans and Austrians of around 5,000 volunteers in total, the French and Italians appear in statistics with a lower percentage of casualties, 1,003 deaths of a total of 8,500 combatants, and 662 of more than 3,000, respectively; although the latter had a very high percentage of injuries, equivalent to 62% of the force deployed. The report prepared by the League of Nations in the French refugee camps in January 1939 offered the number of 12,673 brigadists, of which 3,160 were admitted to hospital. Other sources say that after the dissolution of the International Brigades only 4,640 men left Spain, and that, in January 1939, from 5 to 6,000 foreign volunteers remained on Republican soil, incessantly fighting during the resistance of Catalonia until February of the following year. In December 1938, the Relief Committee for Prisoners of the Spanish Civil War published a "white paper" in France, completed in 1939 with an ap-

▲ Marcel Sagnier (left) and Boris Guimpel (right), commander and chief of Staff of the XIV 'La Marseillaise' Brigade, photographed in the autumn of 1937. Sagnier can be seen with the Republican Army uniform. Even Guimpel wears the main distinctives, but carries an out-of-service gear, consisting of a sahariana jacket, wide trousers, and shoes with leather leggings, similar to the American Army M1917. Sagnier was promoted to the rank of colonel and led the brigade until March 1938 when he was the victim of a car accident. Guimpel, an architect of Russian origin, would later become one of the leaders of the French resistance in the south during the Second World War. (Author's archive)

▼ Another insignia used by Polish volunteers before the establishment of the International Brigades. This flag was brought by the members of the formation formed in Barcelona between August and September 1936 and added to the Sozzi Centuria. The background is red, and the inscriptions, yellow.

hijos del pueblo

batallón Dombrowsky

◂ Soldiers of the XII Brigade in a trench in the Brunete sector, June 1937. Note the wide range of helmets: The Spanish model of 1926, the Adrian and the Czechoslovakian M1930, in addition to pasamontañas and wool caps, as evidence of the existence of disparities in the International Brigades as well as logistical difficulties in the Republican Army. (Author's archive)

▾ Schmeisser MP28 9mm "Naranjero" submachine gun. Built under license in Valencia in the workshops of Alberique, which assigned it this curious name -meaning "orange tree"- was one of the most popular assault rifles in militia formations, especially in the CNT-FAI. All metal parts in dark steel, and wood, varnished and painted with dark shades. Wingspan of 82 cm, and empty weight of 4 kg.

pendix. The Committee, which managed to obtain the release of 100 British volunteers, 95 French, 85 Canadians, and 11 Swiss, stated that in February 1939, 286 prisoners of the International Brigades were in Nationalists hands, 124 Germans and Austrian, 32 French, 28 Poles, 25 Italians; 16 Americans, 14 Swedes, 12 Norwegians, 9 Czechoslovakian, 9 Danes, 5 Yugoslavs, 4 Estonians, 3 Argentineans, 1 Bulgarian, 1 Chinese, 1 Cuban, 1 Romanian, and 1 Mexican. The first name on the list was that of the French Captain Agard, former commander of an international artillery battery of the 35th Division. None of these prisoners were released and their fate remained in many cases unknown. To obtain a sociological framework of the Brigades' volunteers, concerning their age, occupation, and political beliefs, it might be useful to compare the figures of the French contingent, which, among other reasons, was the most numerous.

According to research carried out on a sample of more than 9,000 volunteers, more than half were young people between 26 and 34 years of age, mostly single, and working-class employees, with a clear predominance of workers. Compared to other professions, farmers and workers accounted for 65% of the total, to which 17% of artisans and other self-employed workers should be added.

Politically, at least, two-thirds were Communists or considered as such, and it is undoubtedly one of the highest percentages of all international forces, compared to the British and the Poles. Among the simple combatants, 52% had joined the PCF and the percentage grew to 68% among non-commissioned officers and 79% among young soldiers. Among the company leaders and political commissars, the membership of the Communist Party seems an almost obligatory requirement. The percentages related to Italian volunteers are, according to Pietro Ramella, 38.3% of Communists, 9.7% of Anarchists, 6.6% of Socialists, 1.6% of Republicans, 1.2% of Giustizia e Libertà, and 42.6% of unknown political affiliation. In short, therefore, the presence of Communists would not seem so prevalent and would confirm that almost half of the volunteers of the International Brigades would have come to Spain for reasons other than the obedience of a party discipline. It is equally significant that, among American volunteers, where the local Communist Party acted as the main promoter of the influx of men, convinced Communists did not represent a majority. Certainly, it was also a direct consequence of the relative consensus that Marxism-Leninism exerted beyond the Atlantic, but, however, confirms that the motivations that led them to enlist were the most varied and that, generally, it was the aversion to Fascism the adhesive that joined most of the volunteers. Some historians have insisted deeply on the following equation: a young and unemployed international volunteer, arguing that the participation in the Civil War was an option chosen by the majority of those who had neither a job nor a family to maintain.

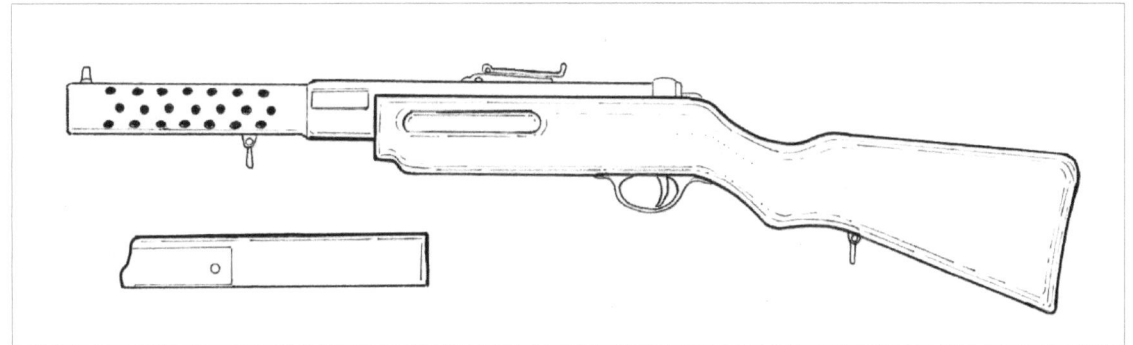

▲ Nino Nanetti (1906-1937), along with Aldo Morandi, was the only Italian to obtain the command of a division of the Republican Army, but, unlike his compatriot, never was part of the International Brigades, and his activism in the Civil War took place completely within the militia and, later, within Popular Army formations. From December 1936, Nanetti led the 35th Mixed Brigade, and then the 12th Spanish Division during the Battle of Guadalajara. Later he was in command of a division in the Basque Country. Nanetti died of a wound received in the defence of Santander in July 1937. Other Italians served outside the international formations in Army, aviation and Navy units. Others served in the War Industry, health, transport, or as translators. (Author's archive)

Apart from the reliable statements of "protagonists" like Randolfo Pacciardi, who wrote that in the Garibaldi Brigade there were no very young, but mature men who had left behind a family and a job, the most recent analyses show that most of the volunteers were between 26 and 35 years old and approximately two thirds were fixed employees. Returning to the analysis conducted on American volunteers, only 25% were unemployed at the time of the arrival, while 30% were professors or university students, which probably makes the American contingent the youngest among the International Brigades, with almost 70% of its members between 20 and 29 years. The fate of those who returned was different according to the country of origin and the role played in the Brigades, but at large, Civil War volunteers had to face many problems once they left Spain. Apart from the few who played an important role in World War II, such as Karol Świerczewski, many of the officers and soldiers transferred to the Soviet Union had to be conformed to secondary positions, as happened to Francesco Leone, while others disappeared into the Stalinist purges, as in the cases of Manfred Stern and Vladimir Čopic. For most volunteers who could not return to their home countries, a long and difficult odyssey began, which in many cases ended in Nazi concentration camps. Others fell fighting in the French and Italian resistance columns. The fortunate witnessed the defeat of Nazism and Fascism, and finally returned to their countries, where, in many cases, a fateful future awaited them. But even those who were able to return freely to their homes at the end of the war had to face several lamentations. American volunteers were under strict FBI surveillance, and many were harassed during McCarthyism. Because of a law of the Swiss Confederation, which banned military service abroad, 420 sentences were applied to ex-combatants of the Civil War, with a prison sentence of up to four years, a real mockery for the citizens of a country that for centuries had provided soldiers all over Europe. Only in 2002, after numerous failed attempts, the Swiss Parliament voted for an amnesty and repealed the sentence for volunteers still alive. In France, the equalization of Civil War volunteers to the rank of resistance veterans became state law only in 1996, after other petitions had been rejected in previous years.

That same year, the Spanish Parliament honoured the promise made 58 years ago by the Republican Government: that once the International Brigades had been dissolved, and the end of the war had been declared, the foreign volunteers who had applied for Spanish citizenship would obtain it, and that having them as fellow citizens would be, for Spain, a complete honour.

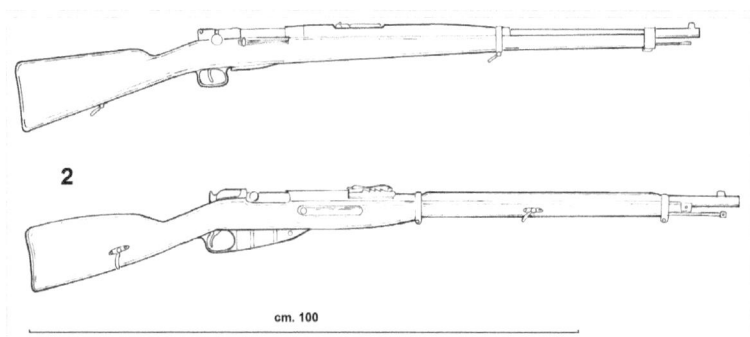

◀ M1893 Mauser 7 mm rifle (Spanish Mauser). Built under license in Spain, it had been the Spanish Army official rifle since 1893 and continued to be one of the most common during the Civil War, used by both sides. All metal parts are in dark steel, with natural painted wood. Length, 124.44 cm, Weight without bayonet, 3.99 kg. The bayonet, with a full handle and forearm, measures 30.48 cm.

◀◀ M1891 Mosin-Nagant Mexicansky 7.62 mm rifle. It was a copy of the Russian imperial infantry rifle made by the United States in 1914. Later it arrived in Spain via Mexico, hence the name that made him popular. It was distributed in large quantities in the International Brigades from January 1937, and was employed until the end of the conflict. It was an effective weapon and relatively easy to maintain, but it was one of the heaviest rifles, with 4.28 kg, as well as cumbersome, with 130.06 cm that, with bayonet, reached 173. The Mexicansky differed from the original model by the tone of the wood, very dark.

▲ The front speaker, one of the popular loudspeaker vans frequently used in the Republican Army to incite fighters and propagate proclamations. The political commissars of the formations had the task of speaking by the microphone, but in general this task was not very welcome, because the adversaries tended to direct the artillery fire in the direction where the voice came from. In Guadalajara, however, the speakers of the Garibaldi Battalion exerted a notable influence on the morale of the Corpo Truppe Volontarie, according to some captive soldiers, who, on learning that there were other Italians in front of them, literally dropped their weapons. (Author's archive)

► Aldo Morandi, alias Riccardo Formica (1896-1975), was one of the few Italian volunteers who reached one of the highest degrees of the Popular Army, obtaining the command of the 63rd Division in the Front of Aragón in October 1937, after having held the position of instructor of the battalion of recruits, chief of Staff, and commander within the International Brigades. Morandi can be seen wearing a short jacket above the Republican Army uniform and wears a isabelino cap with red wool tassel, the typical Spanish Army fatigue cap, with a lieutenant colonel Insignia. The cavalry trousers were very popular among the officers and varied from all shades of brown and khaki. (Author's archive)

▲ Map of the International Brigades' bases and operations (map by Joel Bellviure)

▼ A group of Italian volunteers from the International Brigades in the French refugee camp of Gurs. In December 1938, the League of Nations recorded in the various French concentration camps the presence of 14,936 foreign combatants of the Civil War, of which 1,533 declared themselves Italians. (Courtesy of the Instituto Storico Grossetano della Resistenza e dell'Età Contemporanea)

▶ A group of volunteers, militiamen, and women fighters in a Renault truck during the first phase of the war in July 1936. The militia woman holds in her hand an Astra 400 pistol.

▼ Republican infantry prepares to cross the Ebro (or Ebre) River on the morning of the first day of the offensive in July 1938. "Summer" status of volunteers is also evident by the absence of helmets. The XIV was the first international brigade to cross the river and assaulted some of the most strengthened enemy positions between Amposta and Campredó, losing hundreds of men to conquer a few kilometres from the bridgehead. For the desperate value shown in the Ebre, the Commune de Paris Battalion was awarded a medal of courage. (Image from a newsreel, author's archive)

▼▶ Armed militia poses on top of a 155mm How, Mod. Schneider, Barcelona, August 1936. *(NAC Archive)*

◂ Men from the Edgar André Battalion of the International Brigades in their front barracks, 1936. (Deutsches Bundesarchiv Bild 183-H28510 1936)

---

35 División Internaciónal (december 1937)
Commander: Mayr General Walter (Karol Swierczewski)

- Mayr staff division:
Transmisiones - Aprovisionamiento y logística - Cavalry squadron - Battalion de pioneros - Battery antitanque - Pelotón blindado - Comando de Artillería Divisional (Grupo Skoda Pauker)

        Battery *Agard*   Battery *Francobelga*   Battery *Pasionaria*   XXXII Brigade Mixta (española) 4 batt.

XI Brigade Thaelmann:
 Comandante: Heinrich Rau
 - Estado Mayr:
Battalion *Thaelmann*: 3 cp. fusileros; 1 comp. ametralladoras
Battalion *Edgar André*: 3 cp. fusileros; 1 comp. ametralladoras
Battalion *Zwölfte Februar*: 4 cp. fusileros;
Battalion *Hans Beimler*: 3 cp. fusileros.

XV Brigade Internaciónal
 Comandante: Jorge Agostino
 - Estado Mayr:
Battalion *Lincoln*: 3 cp. fusileros, 1 comp. ametralladoras
Battalion *British*: 3 cp. fusileros, 1 comp. ametralladoras
Battalion *Mackenzie-Papineau*: 4cp. fusileros;
Battalion *Español*: 4 cp. fusileros;
Battery antitanque *Ingles*.

Source: Michel Alpert: *El Ejército Republicano en la Guerra Civil*; Carlos Engel: *Historia de las Brigades Mixtas del Ejército Popular de la República*; Salas Larrazabal : *Historia del Ejército Popular de la República*.

---

3 División Internaciónal (december 1937)
Commander: Mayr General Manuel Tagüeña

- Mayr staff division:
Transmisiones - Aprovisionamiento y logística - Cavalry squadron - Battalion de pioneros - Battery antitanque - Pelotón blindado - Comando de Artillería Divisional

XIV Brigade La Marsillesa
 Comandante: Marcel Segnier
 - Major staff:
Logística – transporte – sanidad – transmisiones
Battalion *Commune de Paris*: 3 cp. fusileros; 1 comp. ametralladoras
Battalion *André Marty*: 3 cp. fusileros; 1 comp. ametralladoras
Battalion *Henry Barbusse*: 4 cp. fusileros;
Battalion *Six Fevrier*: 3 cp. fusileros;
Battalion *Pierre Brachet*: 3 cp. fusileros;
Battalion *Henry Vuillemin*: 4 cp. fusileros.

XXXIII Brigade Mixta (española)
4 Battaliones

XXXIV Brigade Mixta (española)
5 Battaliones

Source: Michel Alpert: *El Ejército Republicano en la Guerra Civil*; Carlos Engel: *Historia de las Brigades Mixtas del Ejército Popular de la República*; Salas Larrazabal : *Historia del Ejército Popular de la República*.

ORIGIN OF INTERNATIONAL VOLUNTEERS								
Country	A: International brigades					B: Milicia	C: other (1)	A, B e C
Source:	Thomas	Delperrye de Bayac	Archivi Comintern	Varios (2)	Liga de las Naciones (3)			Castells
France	9.000	9.000	8.778	8.800	3.278	1.000	3.500	15.400
Germany	4.900	5.000	3.026	3.700	1744	500	900	5.831 (4)
Italy	3.350	3.100	2.908	3.400	1.533	850	400	5.108
Poland	3.000	4.000	3.034	3.200	1.560	200	900	5.411
USA	2.800	2.000	2.274	2.300	839	80	450	3.890 (5)
Great Britain	2.000	2.000	1.806	1.800	469	70	350	3.504
Belgium	-	2.000	1.701	1.450	432	120	800	2.920
Balkan area	-	4.000 (6)	2.056 (7)	-	667 (6)	180	350	2.614 (7)
Sandinavian	500	2.500 (6)	662 (8)	-	434 (8)	-	100	1.177 (8)
Jugoslavia	1.500	-	-	1.400	-	-	-	-
Czechoslovakia	1.500	-	-	1.300	-	-	-	-
Austria	-	-	-	1.200	-	-	-	-
Canadá	1.000	-	-	1.100	377	-	-	-
Hungary	1.500	-	510	1.000	279	-	350	2.148
Cuba	-	-	-	800	-	-	-	-
Holland	700	-	-	700	-	-	-	-
Swiss	-	-	-	650	-	60	-	-
Argentina	-	-	-	500	-	50	-	-
Sweden	-	-	-	500	-	-	-	-
Bulgaria	400	-	-	450	-	-	-	-
Rumanía	-	-	-	300	-	-	-	-
Ireland	250	-	-	250	-	-	-	-
Greece	160	-	-	200	-	-	-	-
Palestina	-	-	-	150	-	-	-	-
Portugal	-	-	-	120	-	-	-	-
Denmark	-	-	-	150	-	-	-	-
Norway	-	-	-	100	-	-	-	-
México	90	-	-	90	-	240	-	-
Cyprus	60	-	-	60	-	-	-	-
Other countries	2.500	2.000	4.482	1.200	3583 (9)	1.100	600	12.526
Total:	35.210	35.600	31.237	36.870	14.936	4.450	8.700	58.796

In addition to those indicated, international volunteers from the following countries also attended: Albania, Argelia, Andorra, Arabia Saudita, Australia, Bolivia, Brasil, Chile, China, Colombia, Costa Rica, Jamaica, Guatemala, Ecuador, Egipto, Estonia, Etiopía, Filipinas, Finlandia, Haití, Honduras, India, Irán, Irak, Islandia, Letonia, Libia, Lituania, Luxemburgo, Marruecos, Mongolia, Nicaragua, Nueva Zelanda, Palestina, Paraguay, Perú, Puerto Rico, República Dominicana, San Marino, Siria, Somalia, Sudáfrica, Túnez, Turquía, Uruguay, Venezuela.

1- Volunteers who served in military health, in aviation, in the Navy, in industry and other military and civil sectors
2- Reconstructions and various sources, such as Marty, Beevor, etc.
3- Registered in France between October and December 1938.
4- Including Austrians. 5- Excluding the Jews, considered separated from Castells, but including Puerto Ricans.
6- Without indication of nationality. 7- Includes Yugoslavs, Bulgarians, Greeks and Albanians.
8- Includes Swedish, Danish and Norwegian.
9- Including 1,521 who declared themselves stateless.

▲ Franco's artillery positions during the first months of the war, West of Madrid, November 1936. (NAC Archive)

▼ The defense of Madrid: An international volunteer observes with her binoculars the operations of the siege of the rebels. (NAC Archive)

COLOUR PLATES (ENGLISH NOTE)

Plate A: 1 – *Centuria Commune de Paris*; French volunteer, Autumn 1936.
Some photos of foreign volunteers show a great variety of dress with several kinds of local made equipment, such as the canvas ammunition pouches, standard issues for this unit formed in Bordeaux in August 1936. This volunteer wears a navy style double breasted coat – possibly of a merchant ship – and civil trousers.

2 – *Grupo Thaelmann*; German volunteer, September 1936.   3 – *Grupo Thaelmann*; NCO, Tardienta, October 1936.
In late summer 1936 this unit marched to Aragon with better dress and equipment than the militia's standard. The first volunteer wears Spanish army kaki cotton shirt, coulisse trousers and gaiters. Regular mod. 1926 steel helmets and fabric *sombreros* of the African Army were the most common headgears. The Spanish Mauser 1895-1913 rifle and the leather cartridge pouches are both Spanish regular army items.

4 – *Grupo Rakosy*, Hungarian Volunteer, September 1936.
Cotton *mono* and *isabellino* headgear are the same clothing worn by the PSUC militia of Catalonia, with which this group was attached in autumn 1936. Many Hungarian volunteers arrived in Spain via USSR, where they had been exiled after the short 'soviet' experience of 1919. Some of the international brigade's major officers, such as Manfred Stern, Janos Galicz and Mate Zalka, were of Hungarian origin too.

Plate B: 1 – *Columna Francisco Ascaso*, battaglione *Giustizia e Libertà*; volunteer, Huesca, September 1936.
Little is known about the dress and equipment of the first Italian volunteers in Aragon, but some evidences shows that they were not much different from local militia. Work trousers and military shirts – maybe from the Italian army in this case – were common in the first weeks of the war. The civilian *borsalino* hat was unusual but it appears as widely used in a picture taken in August 1936. 1b: sleeve badge introduced after the battalion formation.

2 – *Columna Durruti, Grupo Internaciónal*, French volunteer, Spring 1937.
The wool sweater carries a curious badge, possibly alluding to the left alliance of *Frente Popular*. The dark blue *mono* trousers and canvas *alpargatos* shoes are typical in the Aragon militia.

3 – *Columna Francisco Ascaso, Sezione Italiana*; assault group, April 1937. The popular army assault teams were equipped with hand grenades and automatic weapons, like the versatile but dangerous Spanish Schmeisser MP28 *Naranjero*. The hat is typical of the anarchist units in Aragon, known as *Gorra de la CNT*. The frontal badge is speculative.

Plate C: 1 - Battalion *Dabrowski*, 11th International Brigade; rifleman, October 1936;
3 - Battalion *Edgar Andrè*, 12th International Brigade; rifleman, November 1936. The composite range of the international units in Madrid is referenced by photos and eye-witness accounts. Dark civilian-style clothing probably of black-brown leather was common. In the autumn of 1936, Luigi Longo reported that the only available dress for the *Dabrowski* battalion was azure-blue *mono* work suits, worn over the civilian clothing; red kerchiefs were the only distinctive features. The Spanish army leather equipment seems to have been scarce and, instead of regular Spanish ammunition pouches, the volunteers received pale fabric bandoliers. Spanish mod. 1926 helmets and Enfield rifle 0.303 - M1895-1913 were common weapons in the Madrid front.

▲ Republican soldiers part of the infamous "Battalions of Death."
▼ Rebel soldiers in cloaks pointing in their trenches near Navacerrada, during the first winter of war, Sierra de Guadarrama, December 1936.

2 – Political Commissar, 11th International Brigade, November 1936.
The 11th Brigade political commissar Giuseppe Di Vittorio is often portrayed with the heavy lamb wool lined storm coat - known as *canadesa* – very popular among the international brigade's officers in Albacete, worn in many differing patterns. In other pictures Di Vittorio wears kaki *mono* trousers, at least one size larger, gathered at the ankle or free, and a civil cardigan of dark wool. The black French style basque without rank insignia was the common headgear worn by the Italian syndacalist.

Plate D: 1 – Battalion *Hans Beimler*, 11th International Brigade; rifleman Lieutenant, June 1937. A composite of some figures from a group of officers of the newly formed *Beimler* battalion - photographed at the time of the Brunete offensive – he wears a *saharian* light jacket possibly from captured equipment or from the various dress assortments of the international brigades. Breeches from the US Army surplus are worn with legging gaiters. Note the rank insignia on the pocket button.

2 – Battalion *Lincoln*, 15th International Brigade; adjutant, December 1937.
This figure is based on a photo from the American communist Milton Wolf, later major organizer of guerrilla group, who suggested to Ernest Hemingway the principal character for the novel 'For Whom The Bell Tolls'. Wolf wears a mod. 1936 officer's jacket with the rank insignia of Captain on the sleeves and regular Spanish army shirt with tie, hardly contrasting with the informal wool *pasamontaña* headgear.

3 – Battalion *Mackenzie-Papineau*, 15th International Brigade. Political Commissar, October 1937.
A typical campaign dress and equipment of an officer shown in a contemporary photo; note the US army shirt mod. 1917 and the *Sam Browne* style Astra pistol belt.

4 – Battalion *Lincoln*, 15th International Brigade, rifleman.
The *tabardo* coat, here single breasted, without lower pockets for privates was the more common winter clothing of the republican army. The canvas rifle belt is similar to the US Army mod. 1910 seen in contemporary photos.

5 – Battalion *Garibaldi*, 12th International Brigade; machine gunner, April 1937. Another *tabardo* coat, but in the more common double breasted pattern, is worn on a *cazadora*, a short hunting jacket, to improve protection from the low temperature of the *Sierra*. Spanish copies of the French *Adrian* helmets painted in light brown were common in the 12th Brigade.

Plate E: 1 – Battalion *La Marseillaise*, 14th International Brigade; Lieutenant, march 1937.
The *tabardo* coat, shown here without small pockets – possibly acquired from a private tailor – is worn with cavalry breeches and the superb field boots, highly appreciated items which were very popular among the republican officers.

2-3 – Battalion *Mackenzie-Papineau*, 15th International Brigade, rifleman and NCO.
The trench warfare suggested practical insulation to protect the body from the wet and cold. The first soldier wears a tabardo directly on the equipment and the *cazadora* jacket. In the background the observer wears a *capote manta* cloak coat with large cowl under a wax cloth recycled from an old tent.

Plate F: 1 – Battalion *Henry Vuillemin*, 14th International Brigade; rifleman, winter 1937/38. The winter dress of the International Brigades was determined by the shortage of the republican resources and, like other military equipment, came from a wide range of suppliers. The double breasted greatcoats seem to have been more common than the single breasted ones; however, this French volunteer is wearing the second type. The wool *pasamontaña* headgears were sometimes peakless. Note the red three pointed star on the left sleeve, introduced as the International Brigades official symbol after the decree of September 27, 1937.

2 – Bateria *Antonio Gramsci*, grupo Skoda Baller; artillery sergeant, November 1937.
In the republican army the *gorra del plato* cap was worn by officers and NCO without stuffing in so-called Lenin's style; a yellow metal grenade on the cap identified the artillery.
3 – Battallón *Español*, 15th International Brigade, fuciliere, inverno 1937/38;
4 – battallón *Lincoln*, 15th International Brigade; battalion Political Commissar, early 1938. Note the different pattern of the greatcoat collars. The rank insignia for the political commissar included on the cap a gilded metal 'C'.
5 – Battalion *Dimitrov*, 129th International Brigade, rifleman, winter 1937/38.
Strangely some greatcoats distributed in winter 1937-38 seem to have an inverted double breast. Note the leather ammunition pouches of the Spanish Army cavalry, replica of the British bandolier *90 round* mod. 1903.

Plate G: 1 – Armoured car platoon, 11th International Brigade, driver, spring 1937.
Until the end of summer 1937 the 11th brigade deployed a reconnaissance unit equipped with soviet BA-10 armoured car and composed by Austrians in prevalence. The black leather jacket seems to be a local imitation of the Soviet armoured troop's jacket. In a contemporary photo some members also wore Red Army tank helmets.

▲ Members of the 5th Militia Battalion and official soldiers who fought north of Madrid. In the middle, a non-commissioned officer shows a Mauser M1894 rifle.

▶ German volunteers from the XI Brigade marching to the Front of Brunete at the end of June 1937. The first officer on the left is Heinz Priess, later political commissar of the Hans Beimler Battalion. (Deutsches Bundesarchiv Bild 183-Z0806-036)

2 – Soviet Military Consultant, October 1937.
Notwithstanding the Stalin prohibition for the Soviet citizens to enlist themselves in the international brigades, some authors consider the Red Army personnel in the Peninsula as the sixth (or seventh) International Brigade. USSR sent to Spain many officers and NCO, employed as military consultants and instructors, but in some occasions they served in combat roles. The Soviet presence in Spain was around 2.000 men in total, from which 351 were tank crews, 100 artillerymen, 772 aviators, 77 sailors, 352 instructors, consultants and other specialists. With the rank insignia of Lieutenant Colonel, this officer wears the regular 1936 Spanish uniform; note the badge of the major staff – a gilded five pointed star with oak leaves – on the headgear. The standard equipment for officers included an Astra pistol with dark brown leather belt with brass accessories.

3 – *Sección Caballeria Dabrowski*, 13th International Brigade; *Cabo*, maggio 1938.
Small in numbers, but present in five international brigades, the cavalry deployed was never more than one company, employed mainly for reconnaissance and escort duties. The 13th International Brigade was the only brigade to maintain a cavalry unit, formed with volunteers from East Europe - especially Poland and Hungary – until September 1938.

Plate H: Flags

1 – The *Gastone Sozzi* centuria was part of the PSUC militia, named after the young communist from Cesena died by torture in a fascist jail. This flag was carried by the 3rd company's volunteers of *Garibaldi* battalion until the Spring 1937. The obverse was in red but without inscriptions. Approximate size cm. 90x120. (Sources: Archivio of the Ass. It. Combattenti Vol. Antifascisti di Spagna)

2 – This flag was a present for the *Thaelmann* centuria in Barcelona, October 22, 1936, after the bloody fights of Tardienta, where the unit lost its colours. The new flag was given to the Nielsen brothers, three Danish volunteers, who travelled by bike from Denmark to Catalonia. Obverse in red without writings or symbols. Size cm. 105x125.
(Sources: Sebastià Herreros i Agüí: The International Brigades in the Spanish War 1936-1939: Flags and Symbols, Presentation to the 21st International Congress of Vexillology, York, England. July 26th, 2001)

3 – The international volunteers of *Durruti* column carried a flag based on the classic anarchist red and black pattern. Unique example among other confederal flags, this insignia carried hammer and sickle, possibly alluding to the various ideological provenance of the members. Most volunteers came from France, as is evident by the high number of GT-SR union members in the unit *Delegación*, but at least one never identified Italian ex colonel – known as *Pablo* – joined the staff in early 1937. Approximate size: cm. 160x70.
(Sources: CNT-AIT Archives of Camp de Morvedre; Sebastià Herreros i Agüí: The International Brigades in the Spanish War 1936-1939: Flags and Symbols, Presentation to the XIX International Congress of Vexillology, York, England. July 26th, 2001)

4 – This flag is mentioned in the records of some volunteers, who fought in the *Francisco Ascaso* column in the sector of Huesca, Aragon, since August 1936. Unknown size.
(Sources: P. Margheri and M. Puppini, Ricordi di combattenti della Guerra Civile Spagnola, in: Memorie di Spagna, october 2003)

5 – The black flag with skull and bones was yet another source of criticisms for this battalion, raised in August 1936, in Barcelona by Italian anarchists' exiles – who adopted uniform and symbology similar to the fascist ones. An explanation about these choices is that some unit's organizers came from Argentina, where the local anarchist movement adopted a particularly grim symbolism. Approximate size cm. 100x130.
(Sources: Sebastià Herreros i Agüí: The International Brigades in the Spanish War 1936-1939: Flags and Symbols, Presentation to the 21st International Congress of Vexillology, York, England. July 26th, 2001)

6 – The Garibaldi battalion received this flag in October 1936, when it was formed in Albacete and

carried together with other insignias belonging to the early volunteers units, such as the *Gastone Sozzi*. At the early stages, several international units carried flags on red with symbols and writings inspired by the symbolism of the Third International. Approximate size cm. 100x140.
(Source: archive of the Associazione Italiana Combattenti Volontari Antifascisti di Spagna)

7 – From September 1937 the International Brigades carried new flags based on the republican tricolour, as standardized in the popular army. This flag was carried by the fourth battalion of the 13th International Brigade, following the regular army pattern; on the verse was reproduced the heraldic Spanish arm (7b). In some cases the three pointed star occupied the central position on the flag's verse, while on the obverse were carried writings like battalion's denomination and brigade's number. Approximate size cm. 85x150.
(Sources: Sebastià Herreros i Agüí: *The International Brigades in the Spanish War 1936-1939: Flags and Symbols*, Presentation to the 21st International Congress of Vexillology, York, England. July 26th, 2001)

8 – In September 1937 the citizens of Madrid made a present for Albacete base of guidons red-gold-purple with the city's arm and the three pointed star. Similar, but of minor size, other flags were presented for the company of each international battalion. The Jewish company in the Palafox battalion carried on both side the words 'for yours and ours freedom' in polish: *za waszą i naszą wolność* and in Yiddish: פֿאר אײַער און אונדזער פֿרײַהייט װאָ דײַן. Size cm. 50x110.
(Sources: Sebastià Herreros i Agüí: *The International Brigades in the Spanish War 1936-1939: Flags and Symbols*, Presentation to the XIX International Congress of Vexillology, York, England. July 26th, 2001; Germen Zaagsma: *Jewish volunteers in the Spanish Civil War: a case study of the Botwin Company*. London University)

▲ Giuseppe Di Vittorio (second from left), who used the war name of Mario Nicoletti, Albacete, autumn 1936. He was the first political commissar of the XI International Brigade. Next to him is Hans Kahle, chief of the Thaelmann Battalion and future commander of the 45th International Division. The last character on the right is Vittorio Vidali, head of internal counterintelligence, known as "Comandante Carlos". Di Vittorio was one of the first exponents of the Communist Party of Italy to arrive in Spain, actively participating in the organization of International Brigades with Luigi Longo and André Marty. Based in France in 1939, he directed "La voce degli Italiani", an Antifascist newspaper in exile. Arrested in 1941, he was transferred to Italy and interned in Ventotene.

▲ A soldier from the Lincoln Battalion, XV International Brigade, in a drawing by the author, in the winter of 1937-38, protected from the cold with the characteristic wool blanket of the capote style, a garment particularly appreciated and used by many soldiers of the Civil War. The oblique fabric of the cloth guaranteed a good impermeability and, sometimes, especially when the temperature fell below the freezing point, was used over the coat.

▲ Dissolution of an International Brigade, Tortosa, 1938.

▼ American prisoners released in Hendaye, in 1938. They were part of an exchange process of 40 militiamen, in exchange for an equal number of Italian airmen captured by the Republic. The operation was carried out by U.S. Ambassador C. C. Bowers.

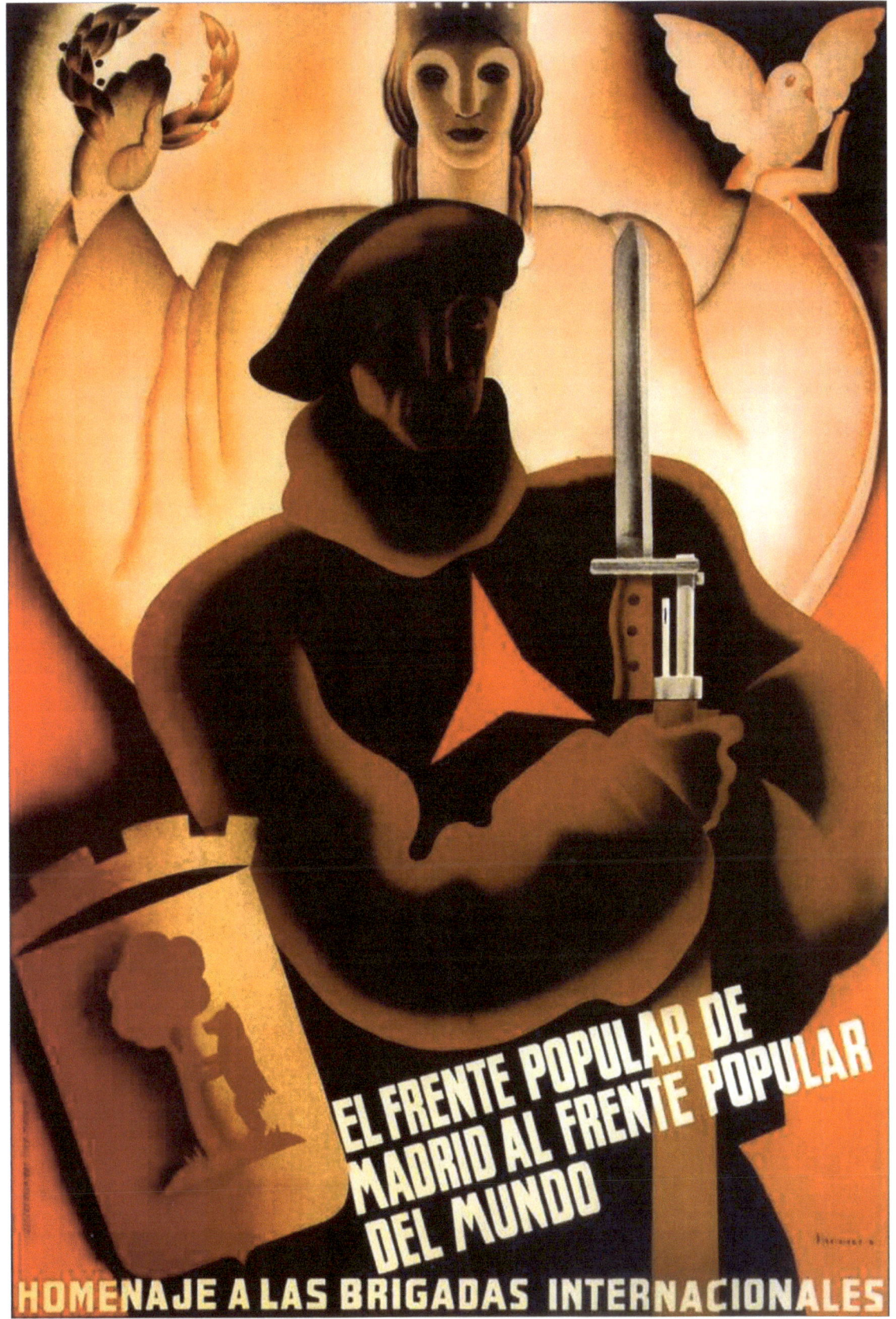

▲ Italian confronted: Italian communist Giuseppe de Vittorio, a volunteer, speaks on Radio España.

▼ Facing Italians: Italian CV-33 tanks of the Corpo Truppe Volontarie commanded by Mussolini, during the Battle of Guadalajara, March 1937.

▲ Dozens of volunteers from the International Brigades arrive on the Cervantes ship from Gijón to Pauillac, near Bordeaux, at the end of the war.

▼ Republican soldiers crossing the French-Spanish border in the Pyrenees, March 1938. (NAC Archive)

▲ Spanish Republican soldiers crossing the border into exile in France in a white 704S truck, their weapons seized by gendarmes, in front of a garage, Le Perthus, 8 February 1939. After Daladier's government decided to open the French borders on January 27, the day after the fall of Barcelona, Le Perthus was one of the most common exile borders in the Pyrenees, along with Junquera, Portbou, Cerbère and Bourg-Madame. As for French uniforms, although in 1935 the French Army had already distributed khaki uniforms, some reservists and non-combatant units still wore the characteristic "horizon blue".

▼ Insignia of the International Brigades Memorial Trust of Limerick (UK). (Luca Cristini Collection)

ESSENTIAL BIOGRAPHY

- CIVIL WAR:
M. ALPERT, A New International History of the Spanish Civil War, Basingstoke 2004.
A. BEEVOR, The Battle for Spain, the Spanish Civil War, London 2006.
B. BOLLOTEN, The Spanish Civil War. Revolution and Counterrevolution, Chapel Hill 1991.
E.H. CARR, The Comintern and the Spanish Civil War, New York 1984.
J.W. CORTADA (a cura di), Dictionary of the Spanish Civil War, 1936-1939, Westport 1982.
R. DE LA CIERVA, Historia de la guerra civil española, Madrid 1969.
R. DE LA CIERVA, Historia ilustrada de la guerra civil española, 2 voll., Barcelona 1970.
J. DIAZ, Tres anos de lucha, Paris 1969.
H. M : ENZENSBERGER, La breve estate dell'anarchia, 1936-37, Milano, 1997.
W. FOSS - C. GERAHTY, The Spanish Arena, London 1938.
G. HOWSON, Arms for Spain: The Untold Story of the Spanish Civil War, London 1998.
S. G. PAYNE, The Spanish Revolution, London 1970.
Idem, The Spanish Civil War, the Soviet Union, and Communism, London 2004.
P. PRESTON, Barricades against Fascism: The Popular Front in Europe, in: History Today, 36,1986.
Idem., La guerra civile spagnola, 1936-1939, Milano 1999.
P. PRESTON (a cura di), Revolution and War in Spain, London 1984.
L. RENN, Der Spanische Krieg, Berlin 1955
R. SALAS-LARRAZABAL, Los datos exactos de la guerra civil, Madrid 1980.
G. SORIA, Guerre et révolution en Espagne, Paris 1976.
H. THOMAS, The Spanish Civil War, London 2003.

-REPUBLICAN ARMY AND POPULAR MILITIA:
M. ACUILAR, El Ejército Espanol durante la II Repùblica, Madrid 1986.
M. ALPERT, El Ejército Republicano en la Guerra Civil, Madrid 1989.
J.M. BUENO-CARRERAS, Uniformes militares en color de la Guerra Civil Espanola, Madrid 1997.
C. ENGEL, Historia de las Brigades Mixtas del Ejército Popular de la Repùblica, Madrid 1999.
J. A. BLANCO RODRIGUEZ, El Quinto Regimiento en la politica militar del PCE en la Guerra Civil, UNED, Madrid 1993.
R. LIÓN - J. SILVELA - A. BELLINDO, La caballerìa en la Guerra Civil, Valladolid 1999.
R. SALAS-LARRAZABAL, Historia del Ejército Popular de la Republica, 4 voll. Madrid 1973.
C. ZARAGOZA, Ejército popular y militares de la Republica (1936-1939), Barcelona, 1983.

- INTERNATIONAL VOLUNTEERS:
AA.VV.: Interbrigadisten: Der Kampf deutscher Kommunisten und anderer Antifaschisten in national-revolutionaren Krieg des spanischen Volkes 1936 bis 1939, Dresden 1966.
AA.VV.: Le Brigate Internazionali: la solidarietà dei popoli con la Repubblica spagnola, Milano 1976.
AA.VV.: Gli antifascisti lombardi alla guerra di Spagna (1936-1939); Milano, Palazzo Marino 7 novembre 1976, Varese 1977.
W. ADRIAENS, Vrijwilligers voor der vrijheid; de belgische anti-fascisten in de Spanse burgeroorlog, Louvain 1978.
L. AGUILERA DURAN, Orìgenes de las Brigades Internacionales, Madrid 1974.
S. AJZNER, Pienvsi Polscy uczestnicy wojny domowej w hiszpanii, 'Kwartalnik Historyczny', 92 (4), Warszawa 1985.
S. ÀLVAREZ, Historìa polìtica y militar de las Brigades Internacionales, Madrid 1996.
J. ÀLVAREZ DEL VAYO, Freedom's Battle, New York 1940.
L. ARBIZZANI, Antifascisti emiliani e romagnoli in Spagna e nella Resistenza: i volontari della Repubblica di San Marino, Milano 1980.
A. BALDINI - P. PALMA, Gli antifascisti italiani in America; 'la Legione' nel carteggio di Pacciardi con altri. Firenze 1990.
G. BAUMANN: Los Voluntarios Latinoamericanos en la Guerra Civil Española, Cuenca, 2009.
A. BENSALEM, Los voluntarios arabes en las Brigades Internacionales: Espana, 1936-1939, Revista Int. de Sociologia, 46 (4), Madrid 1988.
D. BERRY, French Anarchist Volunteers in Spain 1936-39; Contribution to a Col. Biography of the French Anarchist Mov; App. 3; Paris, 2003.
V. BROME, The International Brigades: Spain, 1936-1939, New York 1966.
M. BRON (a cura di), Polacy w wojnie Hiszpariskiej, Wojskowy Instytut Historyczny, Warzawa 1963.
N. CAPPONI, I legionari rossi; le Brigate Internazionali nella guerra civile spagnola (1936-1939), Roma 2000.
R. DE LA CIERVA, Brigades Internacionales, 1936-1939, La verdadera historia, Toledo 1997.
D.D. COLLUM (a cura di), African Americans in the Spanish Civil War, New York 1992.
V. DE CURREA-LUGO, America Latina y la Guerra Civil Española, Bogota, 2003.
R. DAN RICHARDSON, Comintern Army: The International Brigades and the Spanish Civil War, Lexington 1982.
J. DELPERRIE DE BAYAC, Las Brigades Internacionales, Madrid 1980.
M. DERBY, 'Kiwi Companeros', New Zealand and the Spanish Civil War, Christchurch 2009.
D. DIAMANT, Combattants juifs dans l'armée républicaine espagnole, Paris 1979.
A. DURGAN, Freedom Fighters or Comintern Army? The International Brigade in Spain; International Socialism Journal, XI,1999.
Idem, International Volunteers in the POUM Militias, Fundación Andreu Nin, IX 2004.
A EISNER: La 12ª Brigade Internaciónal. Valencia, 1972
K. FINKER, Aufgaben und Rolle des Roten Frontkampferbundes in den Klassenschlachten der Weimarer Rep., in Mil., 13 (2). 1974.
R. FRANCESCOTTI, Sotto il sole di Spagna: Antifascisti trentini nelle brigate internazionali, Trento 1977.

H. FRANCIS, Miners against Fascism. Wales and the Spanish Civil War, London 1984.
H. FRANCIS, Welsh Miners in the Spanish Civil War, Journal of Contemporary History, 5 (3), 1970.
M. GARCIA VJanuary, Historia de los Internaciónales en España, Madrid 1957.
J. GERASSI, Jewish Veterans in the Abraham Lincoln Brigade, New York 1983.
R. GLESS - P. KOLMSEE - B. KOPETZ, Zur Geschichte des Inter. Sanitätsdienstes (SSI) in Spanien 1936-39, Mil., 15, 1976.
V. GUARNER, Cataluna en la Guerra de España, Madrid, 1975.
A. GUTTMAN, The Wound in the Heart: America and the Spanish Civil War, New York 1962.
J. GYORKEI, A spanyolorszagi nemzetközi brigadok egészségugyi szolgalata, in Hadtörténelmi Közlemények, 33 (4), 1986.
P. HUBER, Die Schweizer Spanierfreiwilligen, Zürich 2009.
M. W. JACKSON, Fallen Sparrows. The International Brigades in the Spanish Civil War, Philadelphia 1994.
R. JÄNTSCH, Die militarischen Formationen deutscher Interbrigadisten in Spanien: Militärgeschichte, 15 (3), 1976.
S. HERREROS AGÜÍ, The International Brigades in the Spanish War, 1936-1939: Flags and Symbols, Barcelona, 2003.
V. HOWARD, The Mackenzie-Papineau Battalion. The Canadian Contingent in the Spanish Civil War, Ottawa 1986.
V.B. JOHNSTON, Legions of Babel: The International Brigades in the Spanish Civil War, Harrisbourg, 1967.
C. JØRGENSEN, Danske frivillige i den spanske borgerkrig, in: Arbejderhistorie, (32), 1989.
K. KACZMAREK, Karol Swierczewski-Walter, Militärgeschichte, 12 (5), 1973.
A. KANTOROWICZ., Tschapaiev: Das Battalion der 21 Nationen, Berlin 1956.
I. KEPES (a cura di), Magyar Önketesek a spanyol nep Szabadsagharcaban, 1936-1939, Budapest 1987.
R. KOLAROV, La Sanidad en las Brigades Internacionales, La Mancha, 2006.
A.G. KRYMOV, Manfred Shtern - General Kléber, Narody Azii i Afriki, (1), 1978.
A. LANDIS, The Abraham Lincoln Brigade, New York 1967.
L. LINDBAECK, Internationelle Brigaden, Stockholm 1939.
A. LOPEZ, La Centuria Gastone Sozzi, Quaderno AICVAS n° 4, 1984. Idem, La Colonna Italiana, Quaderno AICVAS n° 5, 1985. Idem, Il Battaglione Garibaldi, cronologia, Quaderno AICVAS n° 7, 1990.
A. LUSTIGER, German and Austrian Jews in the International Brigade, in Leo Boek Institute, Year Book; 35, 1990.
M. MOMRYK, Ukrainian Volunteers from Canada in the Int. Brigades, Spain, 1936-39: Journal of Ukrainian Studies,16 (1-2) 1991.
D. NELLES, 'The Foreign Legion of the Revolution'. German Anarcho-Syndicalist and Volunteers in Anarchist Militias during the S.C.W. 1997.
C.A. NORMAN, The International Brigades in the Spanish Civil War, in Tradition», 66-67, 1972.
M. O' RIORDAN, The Connolly Column, Wales 2005.
N. PALMER (a cura di), Australians in Spain, Sidney 1948.
D.W. PIKE, Les français et la guerre d'Espagne, 1936-1939, Paris 1975.
M. REQUENA GALLEGO (a cura di), La Guerra Civil Española y las Brigades Internacionales, La Mancha 1998.
W. RUST, Britons in Spain: the History of the British Battalion of the XV International Brigade, London 1939.
R. SKOUTELSKY, André Marty et les Brigades internationales, in Cahiers d'Histoire, 67 (2), 1997.
J. SOMMERFIELD, Volunteer in Spain, New York 1937.
B.STEFF Antifascisti di Trieste, dell'Istria, dell'Isontino e del Friuli in Spagna, a cura Associazione italiana combattenti volontari antifascisti in Spagna, Trieste 1974.
R. VAN DOORSLADER, Les volontaires gantois pour les Brigades Internationales en Espagne motivation du volontariat pour un conflit politico-militaire, Cahiers d'Histoire de la Seconde Guerre Mondiale, 6, 1980.
C. VIDAL, Las Brigades internacionales, Madrid 1998.
P. WYDEN: La guerra apasionada. Las Brigades internacionales en la guerra civil española. Barcelona, 1997.

- MEMORIES AND DIRECT FONTS:

AA.VV.: 'Soldiers Return': Letter from an American Fighters in the Durruti Column, New York, 1937, in www.libcom.org
A. BESSIE (a cura di), The Heart of Spain, Veterans of the Abraham Lincoln Brigade, New York 1952.
A. BESSIE, Men in Battle, Scribner's Son, New York 19753.
A. BESSIE - A. PRAGO (a cura di), Our Fight: Writings by Veterans of the Abraham Lincoln Brigade, Monthly Review Press, New York 1987.
G. CALANDRONE, La Spagna brucia; cronache garibaldine, Roma 1974.
J. COOK, Apprentices of Freedom, London 1979.
V. CUNNINGHAM (a cura di), Spanish Front, Writers on the Civil War, Oxford 1986.
L. GALLO (Luigi Longo), Un anno di guerra in Spagna, Parigi 1938.
S. FEDELE, I repubblicani in esilio nella lotta contro il fascismo, Firenze 1990.
M. FELDMAN, Mi guerra de España; testimonio de una volontaria al mando de una columna del POUM, Barcelona 2003.
F. GRIMALDI, P. D'ORAZIO (a cura di), Memorie di una guerra civile, la Spagna del 1936 nelle voci dei testimoni, Roma 2003.
C. HALL, "Disciplinas Camaradas", Four English Volunteers in Spain, 1936-39, Upton 1994.
J. HOPKINS, Into The Heart of the Fire. The British in the Spanish Civil War, Stanford 1998, 270-271.
L. HUGHES, I Wonder as I Wander: An Autobiographical Journey, New York 1956.
J. HUMBERT-DROZ, Mémoires, Neuchàtel 1969-1972.
P.J. JAFFE, Rise and Fall of American Communism, New York 1975.
T. JEREMIC, Studenti Beogradskog univerziteta i jugoslavenski interbrigadisti u francuskim logorima, Istorijski Glasnik, 1-2, 1981.
D. LAJOLO, Il 'voltagabbana', Roma, 2005.
L. LONGO - C. SALINARI, Dal socialfascismo alla guerra di Spagna. Ricordi e riflessioni di un militante comunista, Milano 1977.
I. MACDOUGALL (a cura di), Voices from the S.C.W. Personal Recollections of Scottish Volounteers in Republican Spain, 1936-39, Edinburgh 1986.
P. MARGHERI e M. PUPPINI (a cura di), Ricordi di combattenti della Guerra Civile Spagnola, in: Memorie di Spagna, Associazione

Italiana Combattenti e Volontari Antifascisti di Spagna, X-2003.
J. McGOVERN, Terror in Spain. How the Communist International has destroyed Working Class Unity, Undermined thè Fighi Against Franco, and Suppresses the Social Revolution, Independent Labour Party, London 1937.
R. MALINOVSKI (a cura di), Bajo la bandera de la España republicana, Moskva 1967.
M. MERRIMAN - W. LERUDE, American Commander in Spain; R. Hale Merriman and the A. Lincoln Brigade, Reno 1986.
P. NENNI, Spagna, Milano 1976.
F. F. NITTI, Il maggiore è un rosso, Milano 1953.
G. ORWELL, Homage to Catalonia, London 1938.
R. PACCIARDI, Il Battaglione Garibaldi, Roma, 1945.
G. PAJETTA, Ricordi di Spagna. Diano 1937-1939, Roma 1977.
G. PESCE, un garibaldino in Spagna, Bologna 1955.
Idem, La Spagna nel nostro cuore, 1936-1939, tre anni di storia da non dimenticare, Milano 1996
C. PENCHIENATI, Brigate Internazionali in Spagna, Milano 1950.
P. RAMELLA, Francesco Fausto Nitti, l'uomo che beffò Hitler e Mussolini, in: Il Triangolo Rosso, n° 2/3, 2004.
Idem, I 'diversi' e la guerra di Spagna: la partecipazione di ebrei, neri e omosessuali alla guerra di Spagna, in: L'Impegno, n° 3, 2001
Idem, La guerra di Spagna sui fronti meridionali: brani inediti del diario di Aldo Morandi, in: L'Impegno, n° 1, 2005
H. ROMERSTEIN, Heroic Victims: Stalin's Foreign Legion in the Spanish Civil War, Washington (DC) 1994.
G. SACERDOTI-MARIANI - A. COLOMBO - A. PASINATO, La Guerra Civile Spagnola tra politica e letteratura, Firenze 1995.
I. TAGLIAFERRI, Il colonnello anarchico, Emilio Canzi e la guerra civile spagnola, Piacenza, 2005.
L. ZOCCHI (a cura di), Perché andammo in Spagna. Scritti di militanti antifascisti 1936-1939, Roma 1966.

- **MILITARY OPERATIONS:**
R. COLODNY, The Struggle for Madrid: The Central Epic of the Spanish Conflict, 1936-1939, New York 1958.
O. CONFORTI, Guadalajara. La prima sconfitta del fascismo, Mursia, Milano 1967.
A. CORDÓN, Trayectoria, Ebro, Paris 1971.
J. COVERDALE, The Battle of Guadalajara, 8-22 of March 1937, Journal of Contemporary History, 9 (1), 1974.
G. COX, The Defence of Madrid, London 1937. (2006).
J. HENRIQUEZ CAUBIN, La batalla del Ebro, Mexico 1944.
H. KLOTZ, Les leçons militaires de la guerre civile en Espagne, Paris l937.
J. M. MARRILL, La doctrine militaire française entre les deux guerres, Revue Historique des Armées, 1991 (3).
J. M. MARTINEZ-BLANDE, La batalla del Ebro, Madrid 1988.

◄ The last parade of the International Brigades in the streets of the Eixample in Barcelona, most likely the Diagonal between the 28th October and mid-November of 1938, were the internacionales marched without weapons, in the last act of presence of these soldiers in the Civil War. (From the book "Alert Los Pueblos" by General Vicente Rojo.)

TITOLI PUBBLICATI - ALREADY PUBLISHING

WWW.SOLDIERSHOP.COM   WWW.BOOKMOON.COM

www.ingramcontent.com/pod-product-compliance
Lightning Source LLC
Chambersburg PA
CBHW041543220426
43664CB00003B/36